Table of Contents

v

Chapter 1 - Introduction

C# is the Microsoft's premier language for software development. Microsoft developed C# between 1999 and 2002. In the year 2002, the first version of C# was released to the general public as an integral part of the .NET framework. Since then C# has taken over Visual Basic as the default language of choice for .NET programmers.

C# is one of the most powerful programming languages on the planet. Fully object-oriented and strongly typed, C# is currently being used for web development as backend language for ASP.NET web development framework. It is also widely being as backend language for Windows Forms and Windows Presentation Framework applications. In the world of mobile application development, C# is ruling the Windows Phone development arena.

Salient Features of C#

Following are some of the most important features that make C# so powerful and versatile:

1. Object-Oriented Language

C# is 99.9% object oriented. Like Java, apart from the primitive data types, everything in C# is an object. An object has some properties and can perform some functions. We will see object-oriented programming in detail in a future chapter. For now, just remember that it is the object-oriented programming owing to which C# is modular and maintainable.

2. Strongly Types

C# is a strongly typed language which means that you have to specify the type of data before the program compiles. This is also known as type-safety, which makes C# applications more robust and less prone to run-time errors.

3. Automatic Garbage Collection

In C#, the garbage collection is performed automatically. After a certain amount of time, .NET framework runs garbage collector automatically which removes all the unused objects and dangling pointers from the memory.

4. Easy to Learn

Unlike C or C++, which are considered mid-level programming languages, C# is very high level. Most of the functionalities that require careful handling in C or C++ such as pointers and memory management are handled by default in C#. You can literally set yourself up and write a C# program in less than 10 minutes.

5. *Application Range*

Since C# is Microsoft's premier programming language, almost every Microsoft technology depends upon it. For instance, ASP.NET framework runs C# as backend language, Windows Phone development also utilizes C# and, Windows Form and Windows Presentation Framework (WPF) also depend heavily on C#.

6. *Part of Visual Studio*

Microsoft's Visual Studio is one of the most widely used IDEs in the world and C# is the part of Visual Studio languages which highlights the importance and power of the language.

7. *Huge Developer Community*

C# has a huge developer community. You can get help almost immediately about any problem that you might face during C# development. On www.stackoverflow.com, C# has the 4th largest community. Not to mention that www.stackoverflow.com was also developed using C#.

In short, C# has everything that it takes to become a professional programmer. Enough of the theory, in the next section, we will install the environment that we are going to use to run our application.

Environment Setup

Ideally, to run the C# application, you should have a window machine with .NET framework installed. However, for the starters, I would recommender simply downloading the latest version of Visual Studio, which installs everything that you need to run your C# programs. Visual studio is the first choice IDE for C#.

The latest version of the visual studio can be downloaded here. Once you open the link, you should see the following interface:

Visual Studio comes in three versions: Community, Professional, and Enterprise. The Community version is free of cost while the Professional and Enterprise versions are not free. For the sake of this book, we will only use the Community version. To download the community version, you only need Microsoft account which you can create for free if you do not already have. Visual Studio installation is very straightforward and can be done with few clicks of the mouse.

Running Your First Program

Follow these steps to run your first C# program.

1. Open Visual Studio. You can do so by searching "Visual Studio" at the windows search box as shown below:

2. From the top menu, select File -> New -> Project. Look at the following screenshot for reference.

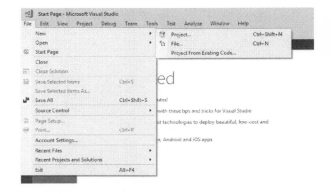

3. You will see a list of different types of programs that you can create with C#. Select "Console App (.NET Framework)", give any name to your application, I named it "MyProgram". Click OK button.

4. You will see a window where you can write C# code. Write the following code in the window

and press the green triangle with label "Start", from the top menu. I will explain what is happening later.

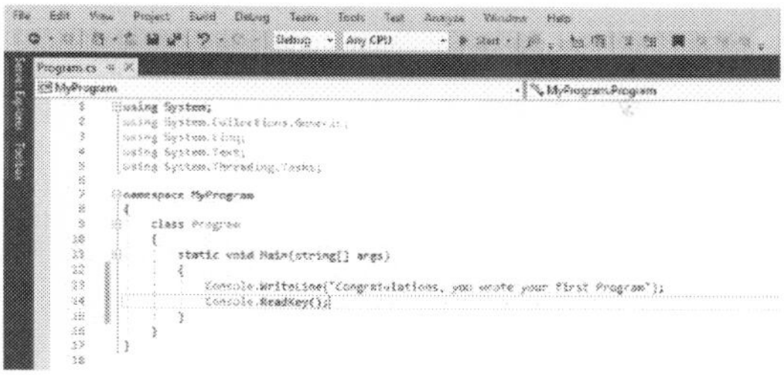

Once you execute the script above, you will see that a console window, like the command line, will appear that will contain the message "Congratulations, you wrote your first Program" as shown below:

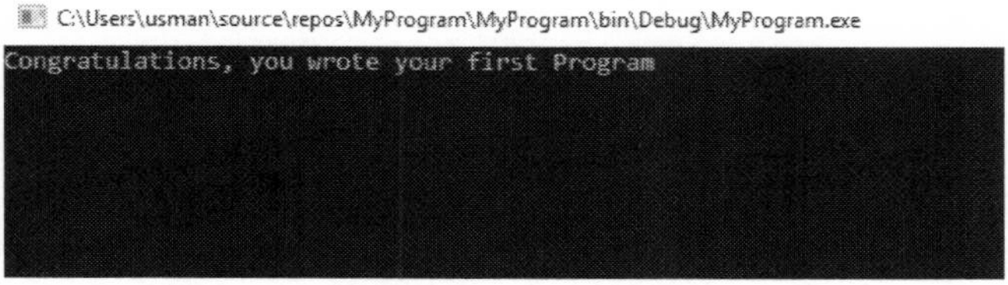

Now let's see what is actually happening. Take a look at the code that we wrote:

```
using System;
using System.Collections.Generic;
using System.Linq;
using System.Text;
using System.Threading.Tasks;
```

```
namespace MyProgram
{
    class Program
    {
        static void Main(string[] args)
        {

Console.WriteLine("Congratulations, you wrote
your first Program");

            Console.ReadKey();

        }

    }

}
```

The *using* statements at the top of the code are used to import any libraries. Libraries are basically set of pre-built functions that we can directly use in our code. Every code snippet in C# has to be inside a class which in turn lies inside a namespace. In the script above our class name is *Program* and it lies inside the *MyProgram* namespace.

Inside the *Program* class, we have method *Main* whose return type is *void* and method type is static. This is the starting point of our code. Do not worry much about the terms *void* and *static* at the moment. We will see these terms in detail in a later chapter. For now, just remember that the *Main* method is the starting point of C# code.

Next, we write a simple line on the screen. To do so, we used *WriteLine* method of the *Console* class and passed it the text that we wanted to display on the console window. Finally, we used the *ReadKey* method of the *Console* class so that our console window doesn't disappear immediately after printing the text. And that's pretty much it. Congratulations on successfully executing your first program.

Conclusion

C# is one of the most frequently used programming languages in the world. In this chapter, we studied some of the salient features of C# followed by the environment setup. To get our feet wet, we actually ran a very small program to see how C# program executes. In the next chapter, we will start our discussion about Data types in C#.

Chapter 2 – Variables and Data Types

Type safety is one of the most important features of C# language. In C#, the type of the data is specified at compile time which makes the application robust. In this chapter, we will see how C# handles a variety of data ranging from numbers to texts and dates to Boolean. However, before that, we will define what is a variable is.

Variable

A variable in C# is a code feature that is used to store data that is changed repeatedly. A variable in C# is similar to the variable in Mathematics to which a new value can be assigned, updated and deleted. Normally a variable is used to store data that is required throughout the application execution time. A type is associated with a variable. For instance, a variable that stores textual data in C#, cannot store numeric data. Similarly, if a variable stores a Boolean value i.e. true or false, you cannot store a numeric or text value to that variable. This is what makes C# strongly typed. A variable is declared in C# by simple prefixing the data

12

type before the name of the variable. T
book, we will make extensive use of the
before that, we need to understand the
types.

Data Types

C# data types have been divided into five categories.
They are as follows:

1. Numeric Types

These types are used to store integer numbers. *They
include int, unint, long, ulong, sbyte, byte, short, ushort.*

The following table shows the value that these integer
type variables can take along with their default values.

Data Type	Default	Min Value	Max Value
sbyte	0	-128	127
byte	0	0	255
short	0	-32768	32767
ushort	0	0	65535
int	0	-2147483648	2147483647
uint	0u	0	4294967295
long	0L	– 9223372036854775808	9223372036854775807
ulong	0u	0	18446744073709551615

oat	0.0f	$\pm1.5\times10_{-45}$	$\pm3.4\times1038$
doubl e	0.0d	$\pm5.0\times10\text{-}324$	$\pm1.7\times10308$
decim al	0.0m	$\pm1.0\times10\text{-}28$	$\pm7.9\times1028$

Let's take a simple example of integer type data.
Execute the following script:

```
using System;
using System.Collections.Generic;
using System.Linq;
using System.Text;
using System.Threading.Tasks;

namespace MyProgram
{
    class Program
    {
        static void Main(string[] args)
        {
            int age = 10;
            long balance = 5464646466;
```

```
        decimal weight = 55.5M;


        Console.Write("Age:" + age + "-
balance:" + balance + "    - weight" + weight);

        Console.ReadKey();

    }

  }

}
```

In the script above, we create three variables *age,*
balance and *weight.* The first variable is integer type,
the second variable is long type while the third variable
is decimal type. We then print the three values on the
console. The output looks like this:

```
C:\Users\usman\source\repos\MyProgram\MyProgram\bin\Debug\MyProgram.exe
Age:10-  balance:5464646466   - weight55.5
```

2. Boolean Type

The Boolean type variables can only have one of the
two values: true and false. Let's take a simple example
of a Boolean variable:

```
using System;
using System.Collections.Generic;
using System.Linq;
using System.Text;
using System.Threading.Tasks;
```

```
e MyProgram

class Program
{
    static void Main(string[] args)
    {
        bool comparison = 10 > 20;
        Console.WriteLine(comparison);

        comparison = 20 > 10;
        Console.WriteLine(comparison);

        Console.ReadKey();
    }
}
```

In the script above we create a Boolean variable *comparison.* The variable can contain only true or false values. We then evaluated an expression where we say that 10 is greater than 20. Since, this is not true, false will be stored in the *comparison* variable and will be printed on the console. Next, we evaluate the expression 20 is greater than 10 which will return true this time and hence true will be printed on the console. The output of the script above look likes this:

```
False
True
```

3. Char Type

The *char* type variable, as the name suggests is used to store the character values. The following example demonstrates this concept:

```
using System;
using System.Collections.Generic;
using System.Linq;
using System.Text;
using System.Threading.Tasks;

namespace MyProgram
{
    class Program
    {
        static void Main(string[] args)
        {

            char sign = '+';
            char bloodgroup = 'O';

            Console.Write(bloodgroup);
            Console.Write(sign);
```

17

```
        Console.ReadKey();
    }
  }
}
```

In the script above, we declare two character type variables *sign* and *bloodgrpup*. We assigned some values to these variables and then printed them on the screen. It is important to mention here that a character can only hold a single value. For instance, you cannot assign a value 'O+' at once to one character. You will see an error if you do so. To handle a series of characters, the string type is used.

4. String Type

String type variables can be used to store more than one character. Take a look at the following example:

```
using System;
using System.Collections.Generic;
using System.Linq;
using System.Text;
using System.Threading.Tasks;


namespace MyProgram
{
    class Program
    {
        static void Main(string[] args)
```

```
        {
            string message = "Your blood group
is";
            string bloodgroup = " O+";

            Console.WriteLine(message +
bloodgroup);
            Console.ReadKey();
        }
    }
}
```

In the script above, we declare two string type variables *message* and *bloodgroup.* We then join the values stored in the two string type variables and display their result on the console. It is important to mention here that to join two strings, we can simply use addition operator "+". The output of the script above looks likes this:

C:\Users\usman\source\repos\MyProgram\MyProgram\bin\Debug\MyProgram.exe

Your blood group is O+

5. Objects

The last and final type of variable is the object type variable. The object type variables can contain multiple variables of various data types. The objects can also perform functions. We will see the object types in more details in the Object-Oriented Programming section of this book.

Conclusion

Data types are building blocks of C# programming language. In this chapter, we covered the most commonly used data types in C# along with their examples. In the next chapter, we will start our discussion about operators in C# which is another fundamental programming concept.

Chapter 3 - C# Operators

In the last chapter, we started our discussion about data types in C#. In this chapter, we will study Operators in C#. Operators are an integral part of any programming language. Operators act upon the data to produce some results. The result of the operator depends upon the data and the operator.

C# operators have been divided into 4 major categories, which are as follows:

- Arithmetic Operators
- Relational Operators
- Logical Operators
- Assignment Operators

In this chapter, we will take a look at these operators in detail along with different examples.

1. Arithmetic Operators

Arithmetic operators in C# are used to perform mathematical operations on numeric data. They are similar to real-world arithmetic operators. Suppose, you have two variables $x = 30$ and $y = 20$, the following table demonstrates how different arithmetic operators function.

Operator	Symbol	Description	Example
Addition	+	Adds the two numbers and concatenates two strings	x + y = 50 "Good" + "Luck"= "Good Luck"
Subtraction	-	Subtracts the two numbers	x − y = 10
Multiplication	*	Multiplies the two numbers	x * y = 600
Division	/	Divides the number in numerator by the one in the denominator	x / y = 1.5
Increment	++	Increases a number by 1	x++ = 31
Decrement	--	Decreases a number by 1	x-- = 29
Modulus	%	Divide the two numbers and returns the remainder	x % y = 10

```csharp
using System;
using System.Collections.Generic;
using System.Linq;
using System.Text;
using System.Threading.Tasks;

namespace MyProgram
{
    class Program
    {
        static void Main(string[] args)
        {

            int x = 30;
            int y = 20;


            Console.WriteLine("Addition of " +
x + " and " + y + " : " + (x + y));
            Console.WriteLine("Subtraction of
" + x + " and " + y + " : " + (x - y));
            Console.WriteLine("Multiplication
of " + x + " and " + y + " : " + (x * y));
            Console.WriteLine("Division of " +
x + " and " + y + " : " + (x / y));
            Console.WriteLine("Increment of "
+ x + " : " + (++x));
            x = 30;
            Console.WriteLine("Decrement of "
+ x + " : " + (--x));
            x = 30;
```

```
            Console.WriteLine("Modulus of " +
x + " and " + y + " : " + (x % y));

            Console.ReadKey();

        }

    }

}
```

The output of the script above looks like this:

```
C:\Users\usman\source\repos\MyProgram\MyProgram\bin\Debug\MyProgram.exe
Addition of 30 and 20 : 50
Subtraction of 30 and 20 : 10
Multiplication of 30 and 20 : 600
Division of 30 and 20 : 1
Increment of 30 : 31
Decrement of 30 : 29
Modulus of 30 and 20 : 10
```

It is important to mention here the difference between ++x and x++. If the increment or decrement operator precedes the operand, then the increment or decrement is performed and then the incremented and decremented value is used in the expression. On the other hand, if the increment operator proceeds the operand, the operand is first used in the expression and then incremented. The following script explains the difference.

```
using System;
using System.Collections.Generic;
using System.Linq;
using System.Text;
```

```
using System.Threading.Tasks;

namespace MyProgram
{
    class Program
    {
        static void Main(string[] args)
        {

            int x = 30;


            Console.WriteLine(++x);
            x = 30;
            Console.WriteLine(x++);

            Console.WriteLine(x++);

            Console.ReadKey();
        }
    }
}
```

In the script above, an integer variable x is assigned a value of 30. It is then incremented using ++x and displayed on the screen. You will see 31 printed on the screen. We then again set its value to 30 and then print it on the console using expression x++. This time you will see that 30 is printed on the console since the increment operator was inserted after x. However, after printing the value of x, its value will be incremented. Now again if you print x on the screen, you will see the updated value 31. The output looks like this:

C:\Users\usman\source\repos\MyProgram\MyProgram\bin\Debug\MyProgram.exe
```
31
30
31
```

2. Relational Operators

Relational operators are used to evaluate the relationship between two or more than two variables or constant values. Relational operators normally return a Boolean value. Suppose, you have two variables x= 30 and y = 20, the following table demonstrates how different relation operators function

Operator	Symbol	Description	Example
Equality	==	Returns true if the values on the left and right side of the operator are equal, else returns false	x == y returns false
Inequality	!=	Returns true if the values on the left and right side	x != y returns true

26

		of the operator are not equal, else returns false	
Greater than	>	Returns true if the values on the left side of the operator is greater than the value on the right, else returns false	x > y returns true
less than	<	Returns true if the values on the left side of the operator is smaller than the value on the right, else returns false	x < y returns false
Greater than or equal to	>=	Returns true if the values on the left side of the operator is greater than or equal to the value on the right, else returns false	x >= y returns true
Less than or equal to	<=	Returns true if the values on the left side of the operator is less than or equal to the value on the	x <= y returns false

		right, else returns false	

Take a look at the following example to see relational operators in action:

```csharp
using System;
using System.Collections.Generic;
using System.Linq;
using System.Text;
using System.Threading.Tasks;

namespace MyProgram
{
    class Program
    {
        static void Main(string[] args)
        {

            int x = 30;
            int y = 20;

            Console.WriteLine(x + " is equal to " + y + " = "+ (x == y));
            Console.WriteLine(x + " is not equal to " + y + " = " + (x != y));
```

```csharp
            Console.WriteLine(x + " is greater
than " + y + " = " + (x > y));

            Console.WriteLine(x + " is less than
" + y + " = " + (x < y));

            Console.WriteLine(x + " is greater
than or equal to " + y + " = " + (x >= y));

            Console.WriteLine(x + " is less than
or equal to " + y + " = " + (x <= y));


            Console.ReadKey();

        }

    }

}
```

The output of the script above looks like this:

```
C:\Users\usman\source\repos\MyProgram\MyProgram\bin\Debug\MyProgram.exe
30 is equal to 20 = False
30 is not equal to 20 = True
30 is greater than 20 = True
30 is less than 20 = False
30 is greater than or equal to 20 = True
30 is less than or equal to 20 = False
```

3. Logical Operators

Logical operators in C# are used to perform logical AND, OR and NOT operations. Suppose you have two Boolean es x = true and y = false, the following table demonstrates the usage of logical operators:

Operator	Symbol	Description	Example
AND	&&	Performs logical AND operation between two or more operands. Returns true if all the operands are true, else returns false	x && y = false
OR	||	Performs logical OR operation between two or more operands. Returns true if one of the operands are true, else returns false	x || y = true
NOT	!	Reverses the logical state of the operand.	!x = false !y = true

Take a look at the following example to see logical operators in action:

```csharp
using System;
using System.Collections.Generic;
using System.Linq;
using System.Text;
using System.Threading.Tasks;

namespace MyProgram
{
    class Program
    {
        static void Main(string[] args)
        {

            Boolean x = true;
            Boolean y = false;

            Console.WriteLine(x + " AND " + y
+ " = "+ (x && y));
            Console.WriteLine(x + " OR " + y +
" = " + (x || y));
            Console.WriteLine("NOT " + x + " =
" + (!x));

            Console.ReadKey();
        }
    }
}
```

The output of the script above look like this:

```
True AND False = False
True OR False = True
NOT True = False
```

4. Assignment Operators

The assignment operators are used to assign value of one operant to another. Following are some of the most commonly used assignment operators in C#:

Operator	Symbol	Description	Example
Assignment	=	Assigns the value of operand on right to the operand on left	x = y, assigns value of y to x
Add and assign	+=	Add the value of operand on right to the operand on left and assigns the result to the operand on left	x += y is equal to x = x +y
Subtract and assign	-=	Subtracts the value of the operand on right from the operand on left and assigns	x -= y is equal to x = x - y

		the result to the operand on left	
Multiply and assign	*=	Multiplies the value of the operand on right to the operand on left and the assign the result to the operand on left	x *= y is equal to x = x * y
Divide and assign	/=	Divides the value of the operand on right from the operand on left and assigns the result to the operand on left	x /= y is equal to x = x / y
Take modulus and assign	%=	Take the modulus of the operand on right with respect to the operand on left and assigns the result to the operand on left	x %= y is equal to x = x % y

Take a look at the following example to see assignment operators in action:

```
using System;
using System.Collections.Generic;
using System.Linq;
using System.Text;
```

```
using System.Threading.Tasks;

namespace MyProgram
{
    class Program
    {
        static void Main(string[] args)
        {

            int x = 30;
            int y = 20;

            x = y;
            Console.WriteLine(x);

            x = 30;
            x += y;
            Console.WriteLine(x);

            x = 30;
            x -= y;
            Console.WriteLine(x);

            x = 30;
            x *= y;
            Console.WriteLine(x);

            x = 30;
            x /= y;
```

```
        Console.WriteLine(x);


        x = 30;
        x %= y;
        Console.WriteLine(x);


        Console.ReadKey();
    }
  }
}
```

The output of the script above looks like this:

```
C:\Users\usman\source\repos\MyProgram\MyProgram\bin\Debug\MyProgram.exe
20
50
10
600
1
10
```

Conclusion

Knowledge of C# operators is crucial if you want to learn advanced C# concepts. In this chapter, we studied some of the most commonly used C# operators with the help of different example. In the next chapter, we will see how we can make our C# application interactive by getting input from the user of the application.

Chapter 4 –Getting User Input and Console Output

The main purpose of a software application is to provide some service to the user. An application should be as much interactive as it can be in order to better facilitate the user interaction. One of the ways to make an application interactive is to take input from the user and present an output according to that input. In this chapter, we will study how we can get input from the user and display output to the user using the console window.

Console Window

A console window is a type of command line interface where the user enters commands via keyboards and the output is represented in the form of text on the same console window. Let's first discuss how data can be printed on the console and then we will see how we can get user input using the console window.

Printing Data on Console

There are two ways to print data on the console window. Either you can use program code that produces some content which can then be printed on the console or data can be read from a local file, database or over the network and then printed on the console. There are two main ways to print data on the console in C#: Write and WriteLine function.

The *Write* Function

The *Write* function of the *Console* class prints whatever you pass it as a parameter on the console. Since every object has a string representation, therefore you can pass objects of all types to the *Write* function. Take a look at a very simple example of the *Write* function.

```
namespace MyProgram
{
    class Program
    {
        static void Main(string[] args)
        {
```

```
bool test = true;
string msg = "Hello from C#";
int num = 10;

Console.Write(test);
Console.Write(msg);
Console.Write(num);

Console.ReadKey();
    }
  }
}
```

The output of the above script looks like that:

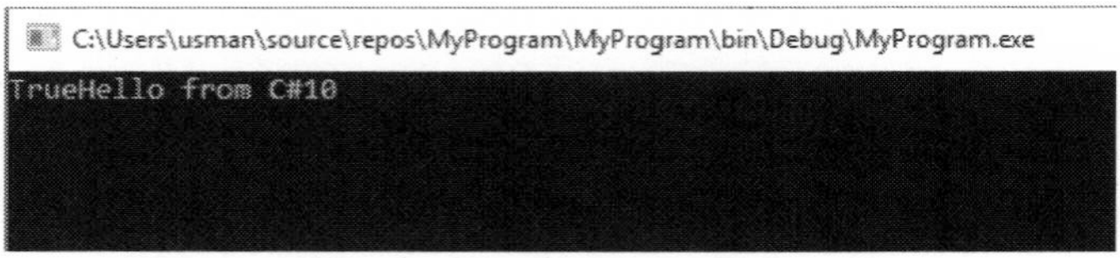

TrueHello from C#10

The output looks strange? Isn't it? All the variables have been printed on the same line without any space. This is how the *Write* function works. It prints the values passed to it on the console and leaves the cursor on the same line. The next *Write* statement will be printed on the same line.

This is where the *WriteLine* function comes handy.

The *WriteLine* Function

The *WriteLine* function on the other whatever is passed to it o a new line. following example:

```
namespace MyProgram
{
    class Program
    {
        static void Main(string[] args)
        {

            bool test = true;
            string msg = "Hello from C#";
            int num = 10;

            Console.WriteLine(test);
            Console.WriteLine(msg);
            Console.WriteLine(num);

            Console.ReadKey();
        }
    }
}
```

The output of the script above looks like this:

```
C:\Users\usman\source\repos\MyProgram\MyProgram\bin\Debug\MyProgram.exe
True
Hello from C#
10
```

Place Holder for Console Output

In addition to directly printing strings in the output, you can also use placeholders that define the position of the corresponding strings in the output. The place holder is defined using curly brackets and inside the curly brackets, you specify the position of the place holder. Take a look at the following example to see placeholders in action:

```
namespace MyProgram
{
    class Program
    {
        static void Main(string[] args)
        {

            string name = "Mike";
            int age = 20;
            string location = "London";


            Console.WriteLine("I am {0}, I am
{1} years and I am from {2}", name, age,
location);


            Console.ReadKey();

        }
    }
```

```
}
```

In the script above, we first define three variables: name, age, and location. We print a string on the console. Inside the string, we use placeholders for the name, age and location. We then simply pass the variables in the same order to the *Console.WriteLine* function, separated by a comma. Here the placeholder {0} corresponds to name, {1} corresponds to age and {2} corresponds to location. The output looks like this:

C:\Users\usman\source\repos\MyProgram\MyProgram\bin\Debug\MyProgram.exe
```
I am Mike, I am 20 years and I am from London
```

Getting User Input

There are multiple ways to get user input through console in C#. We will see some of them in this section.

The *ReadLine* Function

The ReadLine function is used to read complete user input. Take a look at the following example:

```
using System;
using System.Collections.Generic;
using System.Linq;
using System.Text;
```

```
using System.Threading.Tasks;

namespace MyProgram
{
    class Program
    {
        static void Main(string[] args)
        {

            Console.WriteLine("What    is    your
name:");
            string name = Console.ReadLine();

            Console.WriteLine("What    is    your
city:");
            string          location          =
Console.ReadLine();

            Console.WriteLine("Your    name    is
{0} and you live in {1} ", name, location);

            Console.ReadKey();
        }
    }
}
```

When the above script is executed, the user will be
prompted to enter his name. The user will enter his
name and press enter. The ReadLine function executes
which takes the user input and store it in the name

variable. In the same way, the location of the user will be taken as input and stored in the location variable. Finally, both the name and location variables are printed on the console using the WriteLine function.

The output of the script above looks like this:

```
C:\Users\usman\source\repos\MyProgram\MyProgram\bin\Debug\MyProgram.exe
What is your   name:
john
What is your city:
paris
Your name is john and you live in paris
```

Getting Integer Input

Though string type data entered by the user as input can directly be used, integer and other types need to be converted to their corresponding types before they can be used. For instance, if a user enters an integer in response to the ReadLine function, that integer will be considered string. To perform arithmetic operations using that number, it first has to be converted into string type.

Take a look at the following example:

```
using System;
using System.Collections.Generic;
using System.Linq;
using System.Text;
using System.Threading.Tasks;

namespace MyProgram
```

```
{
    class Program
    {
        static void Main(string[] args)
        {

            Console.WriteLine("Enter the first
Number:");
                int    num1    =    int.Parse(
Console.ReadLine());

                Console.WriteLine("Enter        the
second Number:");
                int                  num2                 =
int.Parse(Console.ReadLine());

                int sum = num1 + num2;

                Console.WriteLine("The  sum  of  the
numbers  {0}  and  {1}  is:  {2}  :",  num1,  num2,
sum  );

                Console.ReadKey();
        }
    }
}
```

In the script above, we use the *int.Parse* function to convert the number entered by the user from string to an integer. The user enters two numbers and the sum of the numbers is then printed on the console using the WriteLine function. The output of the script above looks like this:

```
C:\Users\usman\source\repos\MyProgram\MyProgram\bin\Debug\MyProgram.exe
Enter the first Number:
35
Enter the second Number:
30
The sum of the numbers 35 and 30 is: 65 :
```

Conclusion

Getting input from the user and displaying information to the user, are two of the most fundamental programming tasks and are extremely crucial to interactive application development. In this chapter, we saw the basic methods of displaying information to the user and getting input from the user. In the next chapter, we will start our discussion about the conditional statement. Happy Coding!!!

Chapter 5 – Conditional Statements in C#

Conditional statements are programming constructs that are used to alter the execution path of the code depending upon certain conditions. Consider an example where you are asked to build an online ticketing app and you are told that if the user is a student, he should be given a ticket at half price. On the other hand, if the user is not a student, sale the ticket at full price. Here the application is dependent on the condition that if the user is a student or not. Such conditional logic is implemented with the help of conditional statements.

In C#, there are three types of conditional statements:

1. If Statements
2. If-else Statements
3. Switch Statements

In this chapter, we will study each of the aforementioned conditional statements in detail.

If statement

The "if" statement is simplest of the conditional statement. It has two possible return values: true or false. It returns true if the condition satisfies, else it returns false. The syntax of the "if" statement is simple:

```
if(condition == true)
        // execute this
```

Take a look at a very simple example of the "if" statement:

```
using System;
using System.Collections.Generic;
using System.Linq;
using System.Text;
using System.Threading.Tasks;

namespace MyProgram
{
```

```
class Program
{
    static void Main(string[] args)
    {

        Console.WriteLine("Are you a
student? yes/no");
        string student =
Console.ReadLine();

        if (student == "yes")
            Console.WriteLine("You are a
student");

        Console.ReadKey();

    }

}
}
```

In the script above, the user is asked to enter yes or no in response to the question that if he is a student. If the user enters yes, the "if" statement will return true and a line is printed on the console telling the user that you are a student, else the "if" statement returns false and the code inside the "if" statement does not execute, and nothing will be printed on the console. The output looks like this:

```
Are you a student? yes/no
yes
You are a student
```

If-else Statement

The "if" block executes if the "if" condition returns true. What if you want to execute a piece of code when the "if" condition returns false? This is where the "else" statement comes into play. Basically the "if else" statement implicates that if the condition is true, do this, else do that. The syntax of the "if else" statement looks like this:

```
if(condition == true)
        // execute this
else // if condition is false
        // execute this
```

Let's take a simple example of the "if else" statements in action. Execute the following script:

```
using System;
using System.Collections.Generic;
using System.Linq;
using System.Text;
using System.Threading.Tasks;


namespace MyProgram
```

49

```
class Program
{
    static void Main(string[] args)
    {


        Console.WriteLine("Are you a
student? yes/no");
        string student =
Console.ReadLine();


        if (student == "yes")
            Console.WriteLine("You are a
student");
        else
            Console.WriteLine("You are not
a student");


        Console.ReadKey();
    }
}
```

The above example is the extension of the last example. In the above example, we have added else statement to the previously existing "if" statement. Now if the user enters anything other than "yes", the if condition will return false and the else statement will be executed. The output of the script above looks like this:

C:\Users\usman\source\repos\MyProgram\MyProgram\bin\Debu

```
Are you a student? yes/no
```

You can use multiple if and else conditions in your code if you want to check for multiple conditions. Take a look at the following example for details:

```csharp
using System;
using System.Collections.Generic;
using System.Linq;
using System.Text;
using System.Threading.Tasks;


namespace MyProgram
{
    class Program
    {
        static void Main(string[] args)
        {

            Console.WriteLine("Enter your age");
            int age =
Int32.Parse(Console.ReadLine());

            if (age < 20)
                Console.WriteLine("You are in category A");
            else if (age > 20 && age < 40)
```

```
            Console.WriteLine("You are in
category B");
            else if (age > 40 && age < 60)
            Console.Write("You are in
category C");
            else
            Console.Write("You do not
qualify for the offer");

            Console.ReadKey();

        }

    }

}
```

In the script above, the user is prompted to enter his/her age. If the user age is less than 20, the first if condition will return true and he will be prompted that he is in category A. If the user age is greater than 20 but less than 40, the first if statement will return false but the following else if statement will return true and the user will be prompted that he is in category B. If the age is greater than 60, the code after the else block will execute, prompting the user that he doesn't qualify for the offer.

Another very important point to learn from the above example is that multiple conditions can be checked inside if and else if statements. For instance, in the first else if statement we check that the age is greater than 20 and less than 40. Similarly, in the second else if statement, it is checked that the age is between 40 and and 60. A sample result from the above application is shown in the following screen shot:

C:\Users\usman\source\repos\MyProgram\MyProgram\bin\Debug\MyProgram.exe

```
Enter your age
45
You are in category C
```

In addition to multiple if and else statements, you can also have nested if else statements. A nested if-else statement is a statement where if else statement is used another if else statement. The following example explains the nested if-else statements:

```
using System;
using System.Collections.Generic;
using System.Linq;
using System.Text;
using System.Threading.Tasks;

namespace MyProgram
{
    class Program
    {
        static void Main(string[] args)
        {

            Console.WriteLine("Enter your
age");
```

```csharp
            int age =
Int32.Parse(Console.ReadLine());

            if (age < 20)
            {
                Console.WriteLine("You are in
category A");

                Console.WriteLine("Are you a
student");
                string student =
Console.ReadLine();

                if (student == "yes")
                    Console.WriteLine("You are
a student");
                else
                    Console.WriteLine("You are
not a student");

            }
            else if (age > 20 && age < 40)
            {
                Console.WriteLine("You are in
category B");
                Console.WriteLine("Are you a
student");
                string student =
Console.ReadLine();

                if (student == "yes")
```

```csharp
                    Console.WriteLine
a student");
                else
                    Console.WriteLine("You are
not a student");
            }
            else if (age > 40 && age < 60)
            {
                Console.WriteLine("You are in
category C");
                Console.WriteLine("Are you a
student? yes/no");
                string student =
Console.ReadLine();

                if (student == "yes")
                    Console.WriteLine("You are
a student");
                else
                    Console.WriteLine("You are
not a student");


            }


            else
                Console.Write("You do not
qualify for the offer");

            Console.ReadKey();
        }
    }
}
```

In the script, there is a nested if-else statement inside multiple outer if-else statements. The outer if statement checks the age of the user, while the inner if else statement asks the user whether he is a student or not. It is important to mention here that in case of a single line of code, you do not need to enclose your if else block inside curly brackets. However, if you want to execute multiple lines of codes inside an if-else block, you need to enclose your code inside the curly brackets.

One of the possible outputs of the script above looks like this:

C:\Users\usman\source\repos\MyProgram\MyProgram\bin\Debug\MyProgram.exe

```
Enter your age
25
You are in category B
Are you a student
yes
You are a student
```

Switch Statements

Switch come handy when there are a large number of conditions to be checked. The following example illustrates the usage of switch statements:

```
using System;
using System.Collections.Generic;
using System.Linq;
```

```csharp
using System.Text;
using System.Threading.Tasks;

namespace MyProgram
{
    class Program
    {
        static void Main(string[] args)
        {

            Console.WriteLine("Enter your
favourite color");
            string color = Console.ReadLine();

            switch (color)
            {
                case "green":
                    Console.WriteLine("You got
10 points");
                    break;
                case "red":
                    Console.WriteLine("You got
8 points");
                    break;
                case "blue":
                    Console.WriteLine("You got
6 points");
                    break;
                case "yellow":
                    Console.WriteLine("You got
4 points");
```

```
                break;
            case "pink":
                Console.WriteLine("You got
2 points");
                break;
            default:
                Console.WriteLine("You got
00 points");
                break;
        }

        Console.ReadKey();

    }
  }
}
```

The switch statement starts with the keyword *switch,* followed by opening and closing brackets that contain the variable or the value that you want to compare. Inside the switch statement, there are multiple *case* statements. The case whose value matches the value in the switch statement executes.

In the script above, the user is asked to enter his favorite color. The color choice is then stored in the color variable which is passed to the switch statement. Inside the switch statement, each case statement compares its value to the color passed in the switch statement; the case statement for the color that matches the switch statement is executed. The break keyword is used to come out of the switch statement. The output of for the code above looks like this:

```
C:\Users\usman\source\repos\MyProgram\MyProgram\bin\Debug\MyProgram.exe
Enter your favourite color
red
You got 8 points
```

From the output, you can see that when the user enters the color "red", the case statement for "red" executes and the user is prompted that he got 8 points.

Conclusion

Conditional statements are used to execute a piece of code based on a certain condition. In this chapter, we saw what the different types of conditional statements are with the help of examples. In the next chapter, we will start our discussion about the iteration statements or also known as loops.

Chapter 6 – Iteration Statements

Iteration statements or also known as loops are programming constructs used to repeatedly execute a piece of code specific number of times or until a specific condition becomes true. Consider a scenario, where you have to print a statement ten thousand times on console; it will take you ages to write ten thousand Console.WriteLine statements which can be cumbersome. A better way is to use loops. In this chapter, we will study different types of loops or iteration statements in C#.

There are four main types of iteration statements in C#:

1. The for loop
2. The while loop

3. The do while loop
4. The foreach loop

We will study the first three of them in this chapter, we will see foreach loop in the next chapter where we will study C# arrays.

The for loop

The for loop is used to repeatedly execute a piece of code for a specific number of times. If you know the exact number of times that you want your code to execute, you should use a for loop. The syntax of the for loop is as follows

```
for( initialization value, condition,
increment value)
{
        // keep executing
}
```

Let's use the for loop to print the "Welcome to C#" 10 times on console. Execute the following script:

```
using System;
using System.Collections.Generic;
using System.Linq;
using System.Text;
using System.Threading.Tasks;


namespace MyProgram
```

```
{
    class Program
    {
        static void Main(string[] args)
        {

            int i;

            for (i=1; i < 11; i++)
            {
                Console.WriteLine("Welcome to
C#");
            }

            Console.ReadKey();
        }
    }
}
```

In the above script, we execute for loop that starts from 1 (i =1) and will execute until (i < 11) after each iteration or each execution of the code the value of the variable i will be incremented by 1.

As a first step in the for loop, the condition is checked. Therefore, when the for loop starts in the above script it will be checked if i < 11, if the condition becomes true, the code block for the loop executes and the variable i will become 2. However, 2 is still less than 11 and the loop will execute once more. The loop will keep executing until i becomes 11. At that point the condition i < 11 becomes false and the loop terminates. The output of the script above looks like this:

```
■ C:\Users\usman\source\repos\MyProgram\MyProgram\bin\Debug\MyProgram.exe
Welcome to C#
Welcome to C#
Welcome to C#
Welcome to C#
Welcome to C#
Welcome to C#
Welcome to C#
Welcome to C#
Welcome to C#
Welcome to C#
```

Let's do something more complex. Let's print the table of the number entered by the user on the console using the for loop. Take a look at the following script:

```csharp
using System;
using System.Collections.Generic;
using System.Linq;
using System.Text;
using System.Threading.Tasks;

namespace MyProgram
{
    class Program
    {
        static void Main(string[] args)
        {
```

```
        Console.Write("Enter a number: ");
        int num =
Int32.Parse(Console.ReadLine());

        for(int i=1; i<11; i++)
        {
            int result = num * i;
            Console.WriteLine("{0} x {1} =
{2} ", num, i, result);
        }

        Console.ReadKey();
    }
  }
}
```

The output of the script above looks like this:

```
C:\Users\usman\source\repos\MyProgram\MyProgram\bin\Debug\MyProgram.exe
Enter a number: 9
9 x 1 = 9
9 x 2 = 18
9 x 3 = 27
9 x 4 = 36
9 x 5 = 45
9 x 6 = 54
9 x 7 = 63
9 x 8 = 72
9 x 9 = 81
9 x 10 = 90
```

The while loop

The while loop is also used to repeatedly execute a piece of code, however, unlike for loop, which executes a specific number of times, the while loop executes until a specific condition becomes false. The syntax of while loop is as follows:

```
while ( condition == true)
{
/// Keep executing
}
```

Let's use while loop to print a message on the console 10 times. Execute the following script:

```
using System;
using System.Collections.Generic;
using System.Linq;
using System.Text;
using System.Threading.Tasks;

namespace MyProgram
{
    class Program
    {
        static void Main(string[] args)
        {

            int i = 1;

            while ( i < 11)
            {
```

```
            Console.WriteLine("Welcome to
C#");

            i++;

        }


    Console.ReadKey();

  }

 }

}
```

In the above script, we initialize a variable i with value 1. In the while loop condition we check whether the value is less than 11 or not; if it is less than 11, execute the code block for while loop. Inside the code block, a statement is printed on the console and then the value of i is incremented by 1. The loop keeps executing until the variable i becomes is equal to 11. The output looks like this:

```
C:\Users\usman\source\repos\MyProgram\MyProgram\bin\Debug\MyProgram.exe
Welcome to C#
Welcome to C#
Welcome to C#
Welcome to C#
Welcome to C#
Welcome to C#
Welcome to C#
Welcome to C#
Welcome to C#
Welcome to C#
```

Let's see how while loop can be used to print the table of any number as we did in the for loop section:

```
using System;
```

```csharp
using System.Collections.Generic;
using System.Linq;
using System.Text;
using System.Threading.Tasks;

namespace MyProgram
{
    class Program
    {
        static void Main(string[] args)
        {

            Console.Write("Enter a number: ");
            int num =
Int32.Parse(Console.ReadLine());


            int i = 1;
            while (i < 11 )
            {
                int result = num * i;
                Console.WriteLine("{0} x {1} =
{2} ", num, i, result);
                i++;
            }


            Console.ReadKey();


        }
    }
```

```
}
```

The output of the script above looks like this:

```
C:\Users\usman\source\repos\MyProgram\MyProgram\bin\Debug\MyProgram.exe
Enter a number: 5
5 x 1 = 5
5 x 2 = 10
5 x 3 = 15
5 x 4 = 20
5 x 5 = 25
5 x 6 = 30
5 x 7 = 35
5 x 8 = 40
5 x 9 = 45
5 x 10 = 50
```

The do-while loop

The do-while loop is similar to while loop in essence that it also terminates when a certain condition becomes false. However, unlike while, the condition to terminate the loop is checked at the end of the do-while loop after every iteration. This means that the do-while loop executes at least once.

Let's write a message on console 10 times using do-while loop. Take a look at the following script:

```
using System;
using System.Collections.Generic;
using System.Linq;
using System.Text;
```

68

```csharp
using System.Threading.Tasks;

namespace MyProgram
{
    class Program
    {
        static void Main(string[] args)
        {

            int i = 1;

            do
            {
                Console.WriteLine("Welcome to
C#");

                i++;
            }
            while (i < 11);


                Console.ReadKey();


        }
    }
}
```

You can see in the script that while condition has moved
to the end and the do keyword is being used at the

beginning. In the output, you will see a text printed on the console as shown below:

```
C:\Users\usman\source\repos\MyProgram\MyProgram\bin\Debug\MyProgram.exe
Welcome to C#
Welcome to C#
Welcome to C#
Welcome to C#
Welcome to C#
Welcome to C#
Welcome to C#
Welcome to C#
Welcome to C#
Welcome to C#
```

Now let's see how do-while loop can be used to print the table of a number on the screen. Take a look at the following script:

```csharp
using System;
using System.Collections.Generic;
using System.Linq;
using System.Text;
using System.Threading.Tasks;

namespace MyProgram
{
    class Program
    {
        static void Main(string[] args)
        {

            Console.Write("Enter a number: ");
```

```csharp
        int num =
Int32.Parse(Console.ReadLine());

        int i = 1;

        do
        {
            int result = num * i;
            Console.WriteLine("{0} x {1} =
{2} ", num, i, result);
            i++;
        }
        while (i < 11) ;


        Console.ReadKey();


    }

  }
}
```

The output looks like this:

```
C:\Users\usman\source\repos\MyProgram\MyProgram\bin\Debug\MyProgram.exe
Enter a number: 4
4 x 1 = 4
4 x 2 = 8
4 x 3 = 12
4 x 4 = 16
4 x 5 = 20
4 x 6 = 24
4 x 7 = 28
4 x 8 = 32
4 x 9 = 36
4 x 10 = 40
```

The break Statement

The break statement breaks the execution of the loop without executing any further iteration. The following example demonstrates the usage of break statement:

```
using System;
using System.Collections.Generic;
using System.Linq;
using System.Text;
using System.Threading.Tasks;

namespace MyProgram
{
    class Program
    {
        static void Main(string[] args)
        {

            Console.Write("Enter a number: ");
            int num =
Int32.Parse(Console.ReadLine());

            int i = 1;

            do
            {
                int result = num * i;
```

```
            Console.WriteLine("{0} x {1} =
{2} ", num, i, result);

            i++;

            if (i == 6)

                break;

        }

        while (i < 11) ;


        Console.ReadKey();



    }

}
}
```

In the above statement, the table of the number entered by the user is printed. However, when the variable i is incremented to 6, the loop breaks, which means that the table is only printed up to 5. The output looks like this:

```
Enter a number: 6
6 x 1 = 6
6 x 2 = 12
6 x 3 = 18
6 x 4 = 24
6 x 5 = 30
```

The continue Statement

The continue statement sends the control back to the beginning of the loop without executing the remaining code in the loop. Let's print all the even numbers up to 20 using the continue statement. Take a look at the following example:

```
using System;
using System.Collections.Generic;
using System.Linq;
using System.Text;
using System.Threading.Tasks;

namespace MyProgram
{
    class Program
    {
        static void Main(string[] args)
        {

            for(int i = 1; i <21; i++)
            {
                int rem = i % 2;
                if (rem != 0)
                    continue;
                else
                    Console.WriteLine(i);

            }

            Console.ReadKey();
```

```
        }
    }
}
```

In the script above, we loop through the integers from 1 to 20. During each iteration, we check if the remainder of the division of the variable i by 2 is not zero, if it is not zero we do not execute the rest of the loop and come back to the top of the loop. If the variable i is actually divisible by 2, it means it is an even number and we simply print it on the screen.

The output of the script above looks like this:

C:\Users\usman\source\repos\MyProgram\MyProgram\bin\Debug\MyProgram.exe

```
2
4
6
8
10
12
14
16
18
20
```

Conclusion

Iteration statements are one of the fundamental programming concepts. In this chapter, we studied the iteration statements in C#. In the next chapter, we will start our discussion about the arrays in C#.

Chapter 7 – Arrays in C#

In the previous chapter, we started our discussion about different types of iteration statements in C#. In this chapter, we will move a step forward and will start exploring C# Arrays. An array is the most fundamental programming data structure used to store a collection of data.

Imagine you have to store names of 100 students in your class. Without an array, you will have to declare 100 string type variables and then will have to individually store the name of the student in each variable. This can be problematic if you have thousands of records to store. The array is the solution to this problem.

Arrays store collection of data of similar type on contagious memory locations. C# arrays are strongly typed which means that while defining an array, you also have to define the type of data that can be stored in that array. In this chapter, we will study arrays in detail.

Creating an Array

Creating an array, also known as declaring an array is very straightforward in C#. The syntax is as follows:

```
type [] array_name
```

To create an array, you start with the type of the elements that the array will contain followed by the opening and closing square brackets. The pair of square brackets signifies that the variable is an array. After the square brackets, you have to give a name to the array. Notice at this point of time the memory for the array is not reserved. Here you only have defined an array type variable.

To actually initialize an array, the following syntax is used:

```
new type [integer]
```

To initialize an array the keyword **new** is used followed by the type of the array. Remember the type of the array variable and the actual array which is being initialized must match. Finally, the type of the array is followed by opening and closing square brackets that contain an integer value. The integer defines the number of elements that can be stored inside an array.

Let's take a look at a working example of an array in C#.

```
using System;
using System.Collections.Generic;
using System.Linq;
using System.Text;
using System.Threading.Tasks;
```

```
namespace MyProgram
{
    class Program
    {
        static void Main(string[] args)
        {

            int[] years = new int[5];

Console.WriteLine(years.GetType());

            Console.ReadKey();


        }

    }
}
```

In the script above, we create an integer array called years, the size of the array is 5 which means that we can store 5 elements in this array. Next, we print the type of the years variable to see if it actually is an array. The output looks like that:

C:\Users\usman\source\repos\MyProgram\MyProgram\bin\Debug\MyProgram.exe

System.Int32[]

From the output, you can see that the square brackets that follow System.Int32. This signifies that years variable is an array of type Int.

Let's now create another array of type string:

```
using System;
using System.Collections.Generic;
using System.Linq;
using System.Text;
using System.Threading.Tasks;


namespace MyProgram
{
    class Program
    {
        static void Main(string[] args)
        {

            int[] years = new int[5];
            string[] colors = new string[5];


Console.WriteLine(years.GetType());

Console.WriteLine(colors.GetType());


            Console.ReadKey();


        }
    }
}
```

In the script above, we introduced a string type array named colors. Now if you check the type of two arrays you will see that the first array is of type integer and the second array is of type string as shown in the output of the above script:

C:\Users\usman\source\repos\MyProgram\MyProgram\bin\Debug\MyProgram.exe

```
System.Int32[]
System.String[]
```

Instead of using the new keyword, you can also directly create an array by passing the elements of an array inside curly brackets. Each element should be separated by a comma. Take a look at the following example:

```csharp
using System;
using System.Collections.Generic;
using System.Linq;
using System.Text;
using System.Threading.Tasks;

namespace MyProgram
{
    class Program
    {
        static void Main(string[] args)
        {
```

```
        int[] years = { 10, 20, 30, 40, 50
};

        string[] colors = { "red",
"green", "blue", "yellow", "green" };


Console.WriteLine(years.GetType());

Console.WriteLine(colors.GetType());


        Console.ReadKey();


    }

  }

}
```

In the script above, you can see that we directly pass the values inside the curly brackets to initialize the years and colors array. A benefit of using this approach is that you don't have to specify the number of elements that you want to store in an array.

It is important to mention here that C# arrays follow zero based indexing which means that the first element of the array will be stored at index 0. Similarly, the second element will be stored at the first index and so on.

Accessing Array Elements

To access the elements of an array, you need to use the name of the array followed by opening and closing square brackets. Inside the pair of square brackets you need to specify the index of the element that you want to access. Suppose you have to access the second color from the colors array that you created in the last example, you can write the following script:

```
using System;
using System.Collections.Generic;
using System.Linq;
using System.Text;
using System.Threading.Tasks;


namespace MyProgram
{
    class Program
    {
        static void Main(string[] args)
        {

            string[] colors = { "red",
"green", "blue", "yellow", "green" };
            string mycolor = colors[1];
            Console.WriteLine(mycolor);
            Console.ReadKey();


        }
    }
}
```

In the script above we create a string arra
elements. We then store the value of the s
in the array to a variable mycolor. Finally
variable is printed on the console. The second item in
the colors list is string "green", therefore in the output,
you will green as shown below:

Traversing Arrays with the for Loop

If there are a huge number of elements in an array, a
better approach is to use the for loop to iterate over the
array.

Let's see how we can do this:

```
using System;
using System.Collections.Generic;
using System.Linq;
using System.Text;
using System.Threading.Tasks;


namespace MyProgram
{
    class Program
    {
        static void Main(string[] args)
```

```
    {

        string[] colors = { "red",
"green", "blue", "yellow", "green" };

        for (int i = 0; i < 5; i++)
        {
            Console.WriteLine(colors[i]);
        }
        Console.ReadKey();


    }

    }

}
```

In the above script, we use a for loop that that iterates from 0 to 1 less than 5 (5 times in total), during each iteration the iteration variable i, is passed as an index value to the array. This way, all the elements in the colors are accessed one by one. This process is called traversing an array. The output of the above script looks like this:

It is important to mention that if you try to access an element at the array index which doesn't exist, an array out of bound exception will occur. We will discuss exceptions in a later chapter, for now just consider exceptions as errors.

Our colors array have 5 elements, stored from index 0 to 4. Let's execute a loop that traverses the colors array from index 0 to 5 and see what happens. Execute the following script:

```
using System;
using System.Collections.Generic;
using System.Linq;
using System.Text;
using System.Threading.Tasks;


namespace MyProgram
{
    class Program
    {
        static void Main(string[] args)
        {

            string[] colors = { "red",
"green", "blue", "yellow", "green" };

            for (int i = 0; i < 6; i++)
            {
                Console.WriteLine(colors[i]);
            }
            Console.ReadKey();
```

```
                    }

            }

    }
```

In the above script, the for loop runs from 0 to 5, however there is no element at the 5th index of the colors array. Therefore, an error is thrown stating that IndexOutOfRangeException occurred as shown in the following script.

One way to avoid this error is by dynamically setting the range of the array to the number of elements in the array. The length attribute can be used to find the total number of elements in an array. Take a look at the following script:

```
using System;
using System.Collections.Generic;
using System.Linq;
using System.Text;
using System.Threading.Tasks;


namespace MyProgram
```

```
{
    class Program
    {
        static void Main(string[] args)
        {


            string[] colors = { "red",
"green", "blue", "yellow", "green" };

            int length = colors.Length;

            for (int i = 0; i < length; i++)
            {
                Console.WriteLine(colors[i]);
            }
            Console.ReadKey();


        }
    }
}
```

Traversing Arrays with foreach loop

The foreach loop is a loop that iterates exactly the same number of times as the number of items in an array. The foreach loop is the most recommended way of iterating through arrays in C#. Take a look at the following script:

```csharp
using System;
using System.Collections.Generic;
using System.Linq;
using System.Text;
using System.Threading.Tasks;

namespace MyProgram
{
    class Program
    {
        static void Main(string[] args)
        {

            string[] colors = { "red",
"green", "blue", "yellow", "green" };


            foreach (string color in colors)
            {
                Console.WriteLine(color);
            }
            Console.ReadKey();


        }
    }
}
```

In the script above, we use a foreach loop to traverse through the colors array. Pay close attention to the foreach loop part.

For every iteration in the foreach loop, the corresponding array element is stored in a temporary variable which is "color" in the above case. The color variable will hold items from the colors array during each iteration. Inside the foreach loop, we simply print the value of the temporary color variable. The output of the above script looks like this:

```
C:\Users\usman\source\repos\MyProgram\MyProgram\bin\Debug\MyProgram.exe
red
green
blue
yellow
green
```

Multidimensional Arrays

Till now, we have studied one-dimensional array in this chapter, such arrays are called vectors in mathematics. We can have higher dimensional arrays as well. For instance, to create a two-dimensional array in C#, you can use the following syntax:

```
using System;
using System.Collections.Generic;
using System.Linq;
using System.Text;
```

```csharp
using System.Threading.Tasks;

namespace MyProgram
{
    class Program
    {
        static void Main(string[] args)
        {

            int[,] identity = {
                                { 1, 0, 0},
                                { 0, 1, 0},
                                { 0, 0, 1}

                              };

            Console.WriteLine(identity[1, 1]);

            Console.ReadKey();

        }
    }
}
```

In the script above, we create a two-dimensional array which looks like an identity matrix (A matrix where diagonal contains 1 while all the remaining indexes are 0). This is a two-dimensional array. In a two dimensional array, every row is basically an individual array.

To access the element in a two-dimensional array, you have to specify the value for the indexes of both the rows and columns. For instance, In the script above, we access the element from the first row index and first column index. Remember, arrays follow zero based indexing. Therefore, first row index, first column index actually means the element in the second row, second column which is 1. In the output you should see 1 as shown below:

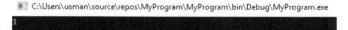

C:\Users\usman\source\repos\MyProgram\MyProgram\bin\Debug\MyProgram.exe

1

Loops can also be used to iterate through a two-dimensional arrays. For each dimension, you will need a dedicated for loop. For instance, to iterate through a two-dimensional or matrix array, you need two for loops. The outer for loop will iterate through each row in the two-dimensional array while the inner for loop will iterate through each element within that row. Let's see how two for loops can be used to iterate through each element in the two-dimensional array. Execute the following script:

```
using System;
using System.Collections.Generic;
using System.Linq;
using System.Text;
using System.Threading.Tasks;
```

```
ace MyProgram
{
    class Program
    {
        static void Main(string[] args)
        {

            int[,] identity = {
                                { 1, 0, 0},
                                { 0, 1, 0},
                                { 0, 0, 1}


                              };


            for (int i = 0; i <
identity.GetLength(0); i++)
            {
                for (int j = 0; j <
identity.GetLength(1); j++)
                {
                    Console.Write(identity[i,
j] + " ");
                }

                Console.WriteLine();
            }


            Console.ReadKey();
```

```
        }
    }
}
```

The GetLength() method can be used to get the number of elements in a specific dimension. You need to pass the index of the dimensions. For instance, to get the number of rows, you can pass 0 to the GetLength() method, similarly for columns, you need to pass 1. The output of the script above looks like this:

```
C:\Users\usman\source\repos\MyProgram\MyProgram\bin\Debug\MyProgram.exe
1 0 0
0 1 0
0 0 1
```

Conclusion

In this chapter, we briefly covered arrays in C#. We saw how they can be created and initialized in C# and how we can access array elements. In the next chapter, we will start our discussion about a more advanced programming concept i.e. Functions. Happy Coding!!!

Chapter 8 – Functions in C#

Function (also known as method) is one of the most important constructs in any programming language. Functions are used to execute a piece of code that needs to be executed repeatedly and has self-contained logic.

Consider a scenario where you have to calculate the percentage of tax on a certain amount. Both the percentage and the amount will be entered by the user. And you need to do this task repeatedly. One way is to write a logic that calculates the tax on the amount every time you need to perform this task. This can be really cumbersome. What if you need to do this 1000 times a day? You will be spending all your day writing such logic. A better approach is to encapsulate such logic inside a function and then implement a mechanism that executes the function and the logic inside it.

In this chapter, we will see how C# functions are implemented, how we can pass and retrieve data from the functions and what the different types of functions are.

Declaring a Function

The syntax for declaring a function is as follows

```
modifier return-type function-name(p1, p2, p3
...)
{
//function logic
}
```

To declare a function, you first have to specify the modifier or access type of function. We will study access modifiers in detail in a later chapter, for now, we will use **public** as access modifier. Public access modifier specifies that our function can be accessed from anywhere. Next, we need to define the return type of the function. The return type specifies the type of the value returned by the function. Next, we need to specify the name of the function followed by opening and closing parameters. Inside the opening and closing parameters, we pass the parameters. The parameters are basically used to pass data to a function. After that, the body of the function is specified inside the opening and closing curly brackets that contain the logic that will be executed by the function.

It is important to mention here that you already have a function named Main whose return type is void (nothing), and which takes an array of string as an argument and is of type static. A static function is a function that doesn't require to be called via an object of a class. We will see objects and classes in detail in a later chapter. For now, just bear in mind that to call a function directly, without object name, we have to use the keyword static.

Let's define a simple function that returns nothing, has no parameters and simply displays some text on the screen.

```
using System;
using System.Collections.Generic;
using System.Linq;
using System.Text;
using System.Threading.Tasks;


namespace MyProgram
{
    class Program
    {
        static void Main(string[] args)
        {

            Console.ReadKey();

        }


        public static void ShowText()
        {
            Console.WriteLine("I am inside a
function");
```

```
          }
      }
  }
```

In the script above we created a function named ShowText() which simply prints some text on the screen as shown by the Console.WriteLine() function. The return type is void and the function is static and public.

Calling a Function

We have successfully created our function, however, to execute this function, we need to call it. Calling a function refers to executing the piece of code that triggers the function.

To a call a function in C#, you simply have to specify the name of the function followed by the opening and closing brackets. Inside the opening and closing brackets, you need to specify the parameters that the function accepts (if any).

Let's call the ShowText() function that we just created from the Main() function. Execute the following script:

```
using System;
using System.Collections.Generic;
using System.Linq;
using System.Text;
using System.Threading.Tasks;

namespace MyProgram
```

```
{
    class Program
    {
        static void Main(string[] args)
        {

            ShowText();
            Console.ReadKey();

        }


        public static void ShowText()
        {
            Console.WriteLine("I am inside a
function");
        }
    }
}
```

In the script above, we call the ShowText() function from the Main function. This is because by default the Main function is executed when a C# program runs.

In the output, you should see the message printed on the console by the ShowText function.

C:\Users\usman\source\repos\MyProgram\MyProgram\bin\Debug\MyProgram.exe

I am inside a function

Non-Static Function

In the previous section, we created a static
the real world, most of the time, we will be
static functions. To access a non-static funct
need to create Object of the class. We will study object-
oriented programming in detail in a later chapter. For
now, just to have a taste of how non-static functions
behave, execute the following script:

```
using System;
using System.Collections.Generic;
using System.Linq;
using System.Text;
using System.Threading.Tasks;


namespace MyProgram
{
    class Program
    {
        static void Main(string[] args)
        {
            Program p = new Program();
            p.ShowText();
            Console.ReadKey();


        }


        public void ShowText()
        {
            Console.WriteLine("I am inside a
function");
```

```
            }
        }
    }
```

In the script above, we made two changes from the last script. First, we removed the static keyword from the declaration of our ShowText() function. Next, inside the Main function, we created an object "p" of the Program class which contains both the ShowText() and the Main functions. Using this object, we can call the non-static ShowText() function with the dot operator. The output looks like this:

C:\Users\usman\source\repos\MyProgram\MyProgram\bin\Debug\MyProgram.exe

```
I am inside a function
```

Parameterized Methods

Parameterized methods are the type of methods that have some parameters. The parameters are used to pass data to the methods. There is no limit on the number and types of the parameters. When the function is called, the values for the parameters are required to be passed with the function call. It is important to mention that the number, order, and type of the parameters in the function call and the function declaration must match.

Let's declare a function that accepts two integer type parameters. The first parameter is the amount and the second parameter is the percentage of the tax on that

100

amount. The function value for the tax percentage and then prints that on the screen. Look at the following script:

```csharp
using System.Collections.Generic;
using System.Linq;
using System.Text;
using System.Threading.Tasks;


namespace MyProgram
{
    class Program
    {
        static void Main(string[] args)
        {
            PrintTax(125, 20);
            Console.ReadKey();


        }


        public static void PrintTax(float
amount, float percentage)
        {
            float tax = (percentage * amount)
/ 100;
            Console.WriteLine(tax);


        }
    }
}
```

In the script above, we declare a function called PrintTax(), which accepts two float type parameters: amount and percentage. Inside the function, the percentage of tax is calculated and printed using the Console function.

In the function call to the PrintTax() function, the values for both the parameters are passed. The value for the amount is 125 and for percentage is 20. In the result, you will see 25 since 20% of 125 is 25 as shown below:

C:\Users\usman\source\repos\MyProgram\MyProgram\bin\Debug\MyProgram.exe

25

Returning Values from a Function

In addition to passing values to the function, we can also return values from a function. To do so, we need to make two changes in our script. The first change is that we need to change the return type of a function from void to the type of value that we want our function to return. The second change is that we need to add *return* keyword in our script which returns the actual value.

Let's see how we can modify the PrintTax() function so that it returns the value of the percentage of tax instead of directly printing it on the console:

```
using System;
```

```
using System.Collections.Generic;

using System.Linq;

using System.Text;

using System.Threading.Tasks;


namespace MyProgram

{

    class Program

    {

        static void Main(string[] args)

        {

            float tax = PrintTax(125, 20);

            Console.WriteLine(tax);

            Console.ReadKey();


        }


        public static float PrintTax(float
amount, float percentage)

        {

            float tax = (percentage * amount)
/ 100;

            return tax;


        }

    }

}
```

In the script above, the return type of the PrintTax()
function has been changed to float and inside the

function the tax variable is being returned using the return keyword. In the output, you will see 25 printed again on the console.

Passing Variable By Reference and By Value

There are two ways that you can pass values to the function parameters: by value and by reference.

Passing by Value

When data is passed to the function by value, the copies of the data passed are created inside the function and the original values are not changed. All the primitive data types are passed by values in C#. Let's see an example of how data can be passed by value in C#:

```
using System;
using System.Collections.Generic;
using System.Linq;
using System.Text;
using System.Threading.Tasks;

namespace MyProgram
{
    class Program
    {
        static void Main(string[] args)
```

```
        {

                int num1 = 10;
                int num2 = 20;


                Console.WriteLine("Numbers before
function call {0} and {1}", num1, num2);
                PrintSquares(num1, num2);
                Console.WriteLine("Numbers after
function call {0} and {1}", num1, num2);


                Console.ReadKey();

        }


        public static void PrintSquares (int
a, int b)
        {

                a = a * a;
                b = b * b;
                Console.WriteLine("Squares are:
{0} and {1}", a, b);



        }

    }

}
```

In the script above we declared two integer variables num1 and num2, we then pass these two variables as a parameter to the PrintSquares() function which takes squares of both the numbers and print them on the screen. In the code above we print the value of num1 and num2 variables before and after passing them to the PrintSquares() function. You will see that the values are not updated. This is because an integer is a primitive type and is passed as values. Inside the PrintSquares() function, a copy of these variables is created and the originally passed values are not updated. The output looks like this:

```
C:\Users\usman\source\repos\MyProgram\MyProgram\bin\Debug\MyProgram.exe
Numbers before function call 10 and 20
Squares are: 100 and 400
Numbers after function call 10 and 20
```

Passing by Reference

When a variable is passed by reference to a function, the actual reference or the memory location is passed to the function. Any update on the reference, causes an update on the originally passed variable. All the custom types are passed by reference in C#. Arrays are also passed by reference. Let's see an example of arrays being passed as reference:

```
using System;
using System.Collections.Generic;
using System.Linq;
using System.Text;
using System.Threading.Tasks;
```

106

```
namespace MyProgram
{

    class Program
    {

        static void Main(string[] args)
        {


            int [] nums = { 10, 20 };


            Console.WriteLine("Numbers before
function call {0} and {1}", nums[0], nums[1]);
            PrintSquares(nums);
            Console.WriteLine("Numbers after
function call {0} and {1}", nums[0], nums[1]);


            Console.ReadKey();

        }


        public static void PrintSquares (int[]
nums)
        {

            nums[0] = nums[0] * nums[0];

            nums[1] = nums[1] * nums[1];

            Console.WriteLine("Squares are:
{0} and {1}", nums[0], nums[1]);



        }

    }

}
```

In the script above we pass an array as a parameter to the PrintSquares() function. Inside the function, we update the values of elements of the array. In the output you will see that the values are updated after the function call as shown below:

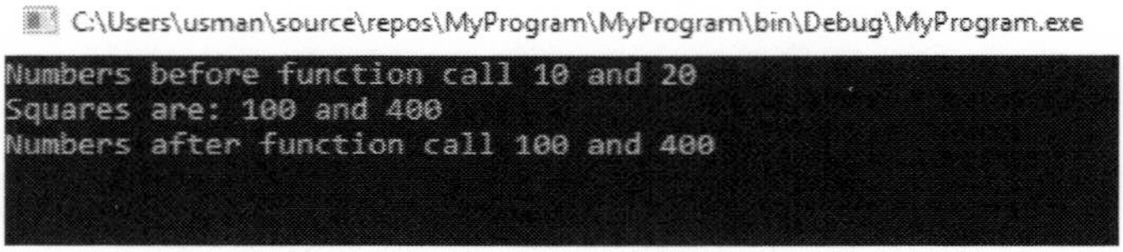

C:\Users\usman\source\repos\MyProgram\MyProgram\bin\Debug\MyProgram.exe

```
Numbers before function call 10 and 20
Squares are: 100 and 400
Numbers after function call 100 and 400
```

Conclusion

In this chapter we covered functions. We saw what the different types of functions are and how to pass and return data from functions. The true power of functions comes from objects which we will see in the next chapter when we start our discussion about Object Oriented Programming (OOP).

Chapter 9 – Object Oriented Programming in C#

In the previous chapter, we completed our discussion about functions in C#. With that, we covered most of the fundamental C# programming concepts. Starting from this chapter, we will switch to more advanced C# concepts. In this chapter, we will start our discussion about Object Oriented Programming (OOP).

It is important to mention that OOP is not a new technology, rather it is an approach to where every component of a computer program is implemented in the form of objects and classes. Consider a scenario where you have to develop a flight simulator using OOP principles. The first task will be to identify the objects in a flight simulator. An object is an entity that has some characteristics and can perform some functionalities. In a flight simulator, the first possible object that should come to your mind is an Airplane. An Airplane has some characteristics such as make, model etc. It also has a few functionalities such as start airplane, stop the airplane, take off, land etc. Therefore it is an ideal candidate for being implemented as an object. Other objects in a flight simulator can be pilots, missiles etc.

It is also pertinent to mention that object-oriented programming is a general programming principle and is not limited to C#. However, in this chapter, we will see how OOP can be implemented in C#.

Advantages of OOP

Following are some of the advantages of object-oriented programming.

• *Reusability*

In OOP, applications are developed in the form of objects and classes. These objects and classes can be reused in other applications as well.

• *Modular Approach*

OOP applications are developed in the form of modules where each module has its own functionality. The modular approach makes application development simple and less complex.

• *Maintainability*

Since OOP applications are developed in the form of modules, it is easy to make changes in one module without affecting the other resulting in maintainable code.

• *Easy Debugging*

OOP applications are easy to debug since an error in one part of the application is usually local and doesn't affect other application areas.

• *Security*

OOP applications focus on data security via encapsulation which we will study in a later chapter. In simple words, the access to data in OOP applications is controlled.

A Class

A class serves as a cornerstone for object-oriented programming. It is a blueprint for the object. It contains information about how an object will look like. How many methods will the object contain, what will be the return type of the method, the type of arguments the method will accept. Similarly, it will also specify the variables that the object will contain. In short, a class is a map for the object. When you see a map, you can easily tell how the house will look like, how many rooms it will have, etc. Similarly, a mere glass at a class can tell what the object is capable of doing and what type of information it stores.

Enough of the theory – Let's see how we can create a simple class in C#. Take a look at the following script:

```
using System;
```

```csharp
using System.Collections.Generic;
using System.Linq;
using System.Text;
using System.Threading.Tasks;

namespace MyProgram
{
    class Program
    {
        static void Main(string[] args)
        {

        }

    }

    class AirPlane
    {
        public string planeMake = "Airbus";
        public string planeModel = "A320";

        public void StartPlane()
        {
            Console.WriteLine("Plane
Started");
        }

        public void StopPlane()
        {
```

```
            Console.WriteLine("Plane
Stopped");
        }


    }
}
```

In the script above, we created a new class "AirPlane" with two member variables "planeMake" and "planeModel" and two member methods "StartPlane" and "StopPlane". To create a class, the keyword *class* is used followed by the name of the class. Next, inside a pair of curly brackets, the member variables and member methods are declared.

It is important to mention here that C# is 100% object-oriented language which means that apart from primitive data types such as string, int, char, everything in C# is implemented as a Class. When you create a new console application, the name of the application becomes the name of the namespace that contains "Program" class. Inside the "Program" class, we have the "Main" method which serves as a starting point for the application. Therefore, if you look at the code above, you can see that we have one "Program" class which is used to start the program and one custom class "AirPlane" that we just created.

Another important point to remember here is the naming conventions. The class and method name is written in Pascal case where the first letter of every word is capitalized. Class variables are written in camel case where the first letter of the first word is small and the first letter of the rest of the words are capitalized.

Now we know how to create a class in C#. However, a class itself has no existence in the memory. An object physically implements a class. Let's see how we can create an object in C#.

An Object

An object in C# is a physical implementation of a class and has a physical existence in the system's memory. An object is also known as an instance and the process of creating an object of a class is known as instantiation. In the last section, we created a class namely "AirPlane", let's see how we can create an object of that class.

```
using System;
using System.Collections.Generic;
using System.Linq;
using System.Text;
using System.Threading.Tasks;


namespace MyProgram
{
    class Program
```

```
    {
        static void Main(string[] args)
        {
            // Creating Object of the Airplane
Class
            AirPlane plane1 = new AirPlane();
        }


    }


    class AirPlane
    {
        public string planeMake = "Airbus";
        public string planeModel = "A320";

        public void StartPlane()
        {
            Console.WriteLine("Plane
Started");
        }

        public void StopPlane()
        {
            Console.WriteLine("Plane
Started");
        }

    }
}
```

script above we create an object named "plane1" of the class "AirPlane". To create an object of a class, all you have to do is use keyword *new,* followed by opening and closing round brackets. The *new* keyword returns the reference to an object which can be stored in any variable.

Now we have a class "AirPlane" and its object "plane1". The next step is to access class members methods using the class object.

Accessing Members and Methods using Objects

To access class members and methods using an object, you can simply use the object name followed by the dot operator (.) and the name of the public member of an object that you want to access. Take a look at the following script:

```
using System;
using System.Collections.Generic;
using System.Linq;
using System.Text;
using System.Threading.Tasks;


namespace MyProgram
{
    class Program
    {
```

```csharp
        static void Main(string[] args)
        {
            // Creating Object of the Airplane
Class

            AirPlane plane1 = new AirPlane();


            // Accessing class members from
plane1 object

Console.WriteLine(plane1.planeMake);

Console.WriteLine(plane1.planeModel);


            // Accessing class methods from
plane1 object
            plane1.StartPlane();
            plane1.StopPlane();


            Console.ReadKey();
        }


    }


    class AirPlane
    {
        public string planeMake = "Airbus";
        public string planeModel = "A320";

        public void StartPlane()
        {
```

```
        Console.WriteLine("Plane
Started");
        }


    public void StopPlane()
    {
        Console.WriteLine("Plane
Stopped");
        }


    }
}
```

In the script above, we use the "plane1" object to display the value of the "planeMake" and "planeModel" variables. Similarly, we also executed the "StartPlane" and "StopPlane" methods by calling them using the "plane1" object. The output of the script above looks like this:

The Constructor

A constructor is a method that executes automatically whenever an object of a class is created. In fact, when you create an object of a class, you use the **new** keyword followed by the name of the constructor. For instance, when we created "plane1" object using the syntax "new AirPlane()", here "AirPlane()"is basically a constructor which is created by default when we created the "AirPlane" class.

A constructor is normally used to initialize class variables. We can override default constructor and provide our own implantation of the constructor. Take a look at the following script:

```
using System;
using System.Collections.Generic;
using System.Linq;
using System.Text;
using System.Threading.Tasks;


namespace MyProgram
{
    class Program
    {
        static void Main(string[] args)
        {
            // Creating Object of the Airplane
Class
            AirPlane plane1 = new AirPlane();
```

```csharp
            // Accessing class members from
plane1 object

Console.WriteLine(plane1.planeMake);

Console.WriteLine(plane1.planeModel);

            // Accessing class methods from
plane1 object
            plane1.StartPlane();
            plane1.StopPlane();

            Console.ReadKey();
        }

    }

    class AirPlane
    {
        public string planeMake;
        public string planeModel;

        public AirPlane()
        {
            planeMake = "Airbus";
            planeModel = "A350";
        }

        public void StartPlane()
        {
```

```
        Console.WriteLine("Plane
Started");
    }


    public void StopPlane()
    {
        Console.WriteLine("Plane
Stopped");
    }


  }
}
```

In the script above, we created a constructor in the "AirPlane" class. Inside the constructor, we assigned some values to the "planeMake" and "planeModel" variables. You can see that the name of the constructor is the same as the name of the class. However, a constructor has no return type, not even void return type. A constructor should always be public since most of the time an object of a class is being created inside another class. The output of the script above looks like this:

```
Airbus
A350
Plane Started
Plane Stopped
```

Parameterized Constructor

Like methods, you can also pass data to the constructors via parameters. Such constructors are called parameterized constructors. Parameterized constructors are handy when you want to initialize member variables with the data passed from outside the class. Take a look at the following example:

```
using System;
using System.Collections.Generic;
using System.Linq;
using System.Text;
using System.Threading.Tasks;

namespace MyProgram
{
    class Program
    {
        static void Main(string[] args)
        {
            // Creating Object of the Airplane
Class
            AirPlane plane1 = new
AirPlane("Airbus", "A-380");

            // Accessing class members from
plane1 object
Console.WriteLine(plane1.planeMake);
```

```
Console.WriteLine(plane1.planeModel);


            // Accessing class methods from
plane1 object
            plane1.StartPlane();
            plane1.StopPlane();

            Console.ReadKey();
        }

    }


    class AirPlane
    {
        public string planeMake;
        public string planeModel;

        public AirPlane(string make, string
model)
        {
            planeMake = make;
            planeModel = model;
        }

        public void StartPlane()
        {
            Console.WriteLine("Plane
Started");
        }
```

```
        public void StopPlane()
        {
            Console.WriteLine("Plane
Stopped");
        }

    }
}
```

In the script above, we have a parameterized constructor for the "AirPlane" class. The constructor has two parameters: make and model, which are used to initialize the two member variables "planeMake" and "planeModel" respectively.

If you look at the "Main" method of the "Program" class, you can see that when we create an object of the "AirPlane" class, we call the parameterized constructor and pass the value for the "make" and "model" parameters for the constructor. The output of the script above looks like this:

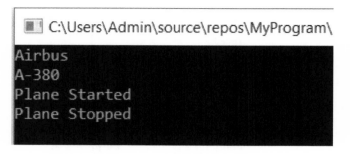

Constructor Overloading

You can have more than one constructor per clas ...ne names of all the constructors will always be exactly the same as the name of the class; the difference lies in the numbers and types of parameters. Having more than one constructor in a class refers to constructor overloading. Let's see this in action:

```
using System;
using System.Collections.Generic;
using System.Linq;
using System.Text;
using System.Threading.Tasks;


namespace MyProgram
{
    class Program
    {
        static void Main(string[] args)
        {
            // Creating Object of the Airplane
Class
            AirPlane plane1 = new
AirPlane("Airbus", "A-380");
            AirPlane plane2 = new AirPlane();


            // Accessing class members from
plane1 object

Console.WriteLine(plane1.planeMake);
```

```csharp
Console.WriteLine(plane1.planeModel);

            // Accessing class members from
plane2 object

Console.WriteLine(plane2.planeMake);

Console.WriteLine(plane2.planeModel);

            Console.ReadKey();
        }

    }

    class AirPlane
    {
        public string planeMake;
        public string planeModel;

        public AirPlane(string make, string
model)
        {
            planeMake = make;
            planeModel = model;
        }

        public AirPlane()
        {
            planeMake = "Lockhead Martin";
            planeModel = "F-16";
```

```csharp
        }


        public void StartPlane()
        {
            Console.WriteLine("Plane
Started");
        }


        public void StopPlane()
        {
            Console.WriteLine("Plane
Stopped");
        }


    }
}
```

In the script above, we have two constructors in our "AirPlane" class, one of the constructors is parameterized while the other constructor doesn't accept any parameters.

In the "Main" method, we create two objects of the "AirPlane" class: plane1 and plane2. The former is created using the parameterized constructor while the latter is created using the simple non-parameterized constructor. The output of the script above looks like this:

```
C:\Users\Admin\source\repos\MyProgram\MyPrograr
Airbus
A-380
Lockhead Martin
F-16
```

Conclusion

Object-Oriented Programming (OOP) is one of the most widely used programming approaches in the world. In this chapter, we studied the basics of object-oriented programming - we saw what OOP programming is, what its benefits are and how classes and objects are created. Finally, we rounded up our discussion with the introduction of the constructor and its types. In the next chapter, we will start our discussion about Inheritance which is one the fundamental pillars of OOP.

Chapter 10 – Inheritance in C#

In the previous chapter, we started our discussion about Object Oriented Programming (OOP) in C#. In this chapter, we will study Inheritance which is one of the three fundamental pillars of object-oriented programming, with encapsulation and polymorphism being the other two.

Inheritance in OOP is similar to real-world inheritance. In the real world, a child inherits some of the characteristics of its parents in addition to having his/her own unique characteristics. In programming, a class inherits characteristics of another class. A class that inherits another class is called child class or derived class. On the other hand, a class that is inherited by other classes is called a base class or parent class.

As a rule of thumb, characteristics that are common in more than one classes should be packaged in the parent class while the characteristics unique to individual classes should be left intrinsic to the individual classes. It is important to mention here that when we talk about characteristics in inheritance, as a programming term, we talk about the member variables and the member methods of a class.

129

Inheritance fosters code reusability and modularity. In this chapter, we will see inheritance in C#.

Inheritance: A Simple Example

Before we see the actual C# code for inheritance, it is important to mention that Inheritance implements the IS-A relationship between the classes. For instance, a car is a vehicle; a bike is also a vehicle. A manager is an employee; a cashier is also an employee. To implement inheritance, the more general characteristics such as name, age, salary can be packaged in a parent Employee class, while more specialized characteristics such as a list of employees being managed can be added to the child Manager class.

In the following example, we will create a parent class "AirPlane" and its child class "CommercialPlane". The parent class "AirPlane" will have member variables planeMake, planeModel and member methods StartPlane and StopPlane. The class "CommercialPlane" will inherit the "AirPlane" class, therefore it will explicitly have the two member variables and the two methods of the parent class. In addition, we will add a variable passengerCapacity to the "CommercialPlane" class. We will also add a method BoardPassenger to the "CommercialPlane" class. We did not add the passengerCapacity variable and the BoardPassenger method to the parent "AirPlane" class since there can be another child class "FighterPlane" and fighter planes do not have any passengers. Therefore, we will implement the passengerCapacity variable and the BoardPassenger method in the child "CommercialPlane" class.

Take a look at the following script:

```
using System;
using System.Collections.Generic;
using System.Linq;
using System.Text;
using System.Threading.Tasks;


namespace MyProgram
{
    class Program
    {
        static void Main(string[] args)
        {
            // Creating Object of the
CommercialPlane Class
            CommercialPlane plane1 = new
CommercialPlane();


            // Accessing parent class members
from plane1 object

Console.WriteLine(plane1.planeMake);

Console.WriteLine(plane1.planeModel);
```

```csharp
            // Accessing parent class methods
from plane1 object
            plane1.StartPlane();
            plane1.StartPlane();


            // Accessing child class members
from plane1 object

Console.WriteLine(plane1.passengerCapacity);


            // Accessing child class methods
from plane1 object
            plane1.BoardPassenger();


            Console.ReadKey();
        }


    }

    class AirPlane
    {
        public string planeMake = "Boeing";
        public string planeModel=  "A330";


        public void StartPlane()
        {
            Console.WriteLine("Plane
Started");
        }
```

```
        public void StopPlane()
        {
            Console.WriteLine("Plane
Stopped");
        }
    }


    class CommercialPlane: AirPlane
    {
        public int passengerCapacity = 180;

        public void BoardPassenger()
        {
            Console.WriteLine("Boarding
Started");
        }

    }
}
```

In the script above we have three classes: "Program" which contains the "Main" method, the parent "AirPlane" class, and the child "CommercialPlane" class which inherits the "AirPlane" class.

You can see that to inherit one class from another, all you have to do is to add colon after the name of the child class and after the colon, you need to add the name of the parent class.

In the above script, in the "Main" method of the "Program" class, an object "plane1" of the "CommercialPlane" class has been instantiated. Next, the values of the variables from the parent class have been printed on the console followed by a call to the parent class method. You will see that the compiler will not give any error since parent class variables are accessible to the child class. After that, the value of the member variable of the child class has been printed and the call to the member method of the child class is executed. The output of the script above looks like this:

```
Boeing
A330
Plane Started
Plane Started
180
Boarding Started
```

Multiple Inheritance

In C#, one-way multiple inheritance is possible, which means that one parent class can have multiple child classes. However, one child class cannot have multiple parents.

In the previous section, we created "CommercialPlane" child class of the parent "AirPlane" class. In this section, we will create another child class named, "FighterPlane" with one intrinsic variable "totalMissiles" and one method "FireMissile". Again, this member variable and method is too specific, hence we cannot declare them inside the parent "AirPlane" class. Take a look at the following example:

```
using System;
using System.Collections.Generic;
using System.Linq;
using System.Text;
using System.Threading.Tasks;


namespace MyProgram
{
    class Program
    {
        static void Main(string[] args)
        {
            // Creating Object of the
CommercialPlane Class
            CommercialPlane plane1 = new
CommercialPlane();


            // Creating Object of the
CommercialPlane Class
```

```csharp
            FighterPlane plane2 = new
FighterPlane();


            // Accessing parent class members
from plane1 object

Console.WriteLine(plane1.planeMake);

Console.WriteLine(plane1.planeModel);


            // Accessing parent class methods
from plane1 object
            plane1.StartPlane();
            plane1.StartPlane();


            // Accessing child class members
from plane1 object

Console.WriteLine(plane1.passengerCapacity);


            // Accessing child class methods
from plane1 object
            plane1.BoardPassenger();



            // Accessing parent class members
from plane2 object

Console.WriteLine(plane2.planeMake);
```

```csharp
Console.WriteLine(plane2.planeModel);




            // Accessing parent class methods
from plane2 object ?
            plane1.StartPlane();
            plane1.StartPlane();


            // Accessing child class members
from plane2 object

Console.WriteLine(plane2.totalMissiles);



            // Accessing child class methods
from plane1 object ?
            plane2.FireMissile();


            Console.ReadKey();
    }

}


class AirPlane
{
        public string planeMake = "Boeing";
        public string planeModel=  "A330";



        public void StartPlane()
```

137

```csharp
        {
            Console.WriteLine("Plane
Started");
        }


        public void StopPlane()
        {
            Console.WriteLine("Plane
Stopped");
        }
    }


    class CommercialPlane: AirPlane
    {
        public int passengerCapacity = 180;


        public void BoardPassenger()
        {
            Console.WriteLine("Boarding
Started");
        }
    }


    class FighterPlane : AirPlane
    {
        public int totalMissiles = 200 ;


        public void FireMissile()
        {
```

```
                Console.WriteLine("Missile
Fired");

        }


    }

}
```

In the script above, we create a plane1 object of "CommercialPlane" class and plane2 object of "FighterPlane" class. We then used both these objects to access their intrinsic methods and variables and the parent "AirPlane" class methods and variables. The purpose of this example is to show how multiple inheritance is implemented in C#. The output of the script above looks like this:

```
■ C:\Users\Admin\source\repos\MyPrc
Boeing
A330
Plane Started
Plane Started
180
Boarding Started
Boeing
A330
Plane Started
Plane Started
200
Missile Fired
```

Calling Parent Class Constructor from Children Classes

In the previous examples, we did not have parameterized constructors for parent and children classes. What if we want to have parameterized constructors for the child as well as parent classes? How will we pass data from child class constructor to parent class constructor?

To do so the "base" function is used and the parent class parameters are passed to this function. In the following example, the child, as well as parent classes, have parameterized constructors. The "base" method is being used to pass data for the constructor from children to parent class.

```
using System;
using System.Collections.Generic;
using System.Linq;
using System.Text;
using System.Threading.Tasks;

namespace MyProgram
{
    class Program
    {
        static void Main(string[] args)
```

```csharp
        {
                // Creating Object of the
CommercialPlane Class
                CommercialPlane plane1 = new
CommercialPlane("Airbus", "A350", 400 );


                // Creating Object of the
CommercialPlane Class
                FighterPlane plane2 = new
FighterPlane("Lockhead Martin", "F-16", 50);


                // Accessing parent class members
from plane1 object

Console.WriteLine(plane1.planeMake);

Console.WriteLine(plane1.planeModel);



                // Accessing parent class methods
from plane1 object
                plane1.StartPlane();
                plane1.StartPlane();


                // Accessing child class members
from plane1 object

Console.WriteLine(plane1.passengerCapacity);



                // Accessing child class methods
from plane1 object
                plane1.BoardPassenger();
```

```
            // Accessing parent class members
from plane2 object

Console.WriteLine(plane2.planeMake);

Console.WriteLine(plane2.planeModel);


            // Accessing parent class methods
from plane2 object
            plane1.StartPlane();
            plane1.StartPlane();


            // Accessing child class members
from plane2 object

Console.WriteLine(plane2.totalMissiles);


            // Accessing child class methods
from plane1 object
            plane2.FireMissile();

            Console.ReadKey();
        }


    }
```

```csharp
class AirPlane
{
    public string planeMake;
    public string planeModel;

    public AirPlane(string make, string model)
    {
        planeMake = make;
        planeModel = model;
    }

    public void StartPlane()
    {
        Console.WriteLine("Plane Started");
    }

    public void StopPlane()
    {
        Console.WriteLine("Plane Stopped");
    }
}

class CommercialPlane: AirPlane
{
    public int passengerCapacity;
```

```csharp
        public CommercialPlane(string make,
string model, int passengerCapacity) :
base(make, model)
        {
            this.passengerCapacity =
passengerCapacity;
        }


        public void BoardPassenger()
        {
            Console.WriteLine("Boarding
Started");
        }
    }


    class FighterPlane : AirPlane
    {
        public int totalMissiles;


        public FighterPlane(string make,
string model, int totalmissile): base (make,
model)
        {
            this.totalMissiles = totalmissile;
        }


        public void FireMissile()
        {
            Console.WriteLine("Missile
Fired");
        }
```

144

```
        }
}
```

The output of the script above looks like this:

```
C:\Users\Admin\source\repos\MyProgram\
Airbus
A350
Plane Started
Plane Started
400
Boarding Started
Lockhead Martin
F-16
Plane Started
Plane Started
50
Missile Fired
```

Conclusion

Inheritance is one of the pillars of object-oriented programming. In this chapter, we started our discussion about inheritance in C#. We also saw multiple inheritance with the help of examples. Finally, we saw how to pass parameters from a child class constructors to parent class constructor. In the next chapter, we will start our discussion about polymorphism which is another extremely important concept of object-oriented programming!

Chapter 11 – Polymorphism and Encapsulation in C#

In the last chapter, we studied inheritance which is one of the building blocks of object oriented programming. In this chapter, we will discuss Polymorphism which is another important concept in object oriented programming. We will also briefly review encapsulation which is considered the third pillar of object oriented programming.

Polymorphism

Polymorphism means having multiple forms. In terms of object oriented programming, polymorphism refers to the ability of an object to behave in different ways.

In C#, there are two ways to implement polymorphism: via method overloading and via method overriding.

Polymorphism via Method Overloading

Polymorphism can be implemented by overloading methods of a class. Such type of polymorphism is known as compile time or static polymorphism, since the logic for method overloading is evaluated at

147

compile time. We have already studied method overloading in a previous chapter.

Let's take a look at a very simple example of polymorphism via method overloading.

Example1:

```
using System;
using System.Collections.Generic;
using System.Linq;
using System.Text;
using System.Threading.Tasks;

namespace MyProgram
{
    class Program
    {
        static void Main(string[] args)
        {
            X x = new X();
            x.MethodA();
            x.MethodA(10);

            Console.ReadKey();
        }

    }

    class X
```

```
{
        public void MethodA()
        {
                Console.WriteLine("This is method
A in class X");
        }

        public void MethodA(int n)
        {
                Console.WriteLine("This is
overloaded method A in class X");
        }

    }

}
```

In the script above, we have a class "X" with an
overloaded method "MethodA". The first version of
"MethodA" doesn't accept any parameter while the
overloaded version accepts one integer type parameter.
Inside the "Main" method, we create object of class X
and call both the original and overloaded version of
"MethodA", in the output you will see that depending
upon the method call, the corresponding definition of
the method will be executed. The example shows
polymorphism in action where actually we had only one
method "MethodA" but depending upon the

parameters, it behaved differently. The output of the script above looks like this:

```
C:\Users\Admin\source\repos\MyProgram\MyProc
```
```
This is method A in class X
This is overloaded method A in class X
```

Let's take a look a more complex example of polymorphism via method overloading. Let's revert back to our "AirPlane" example that we have been using to explain different concepts since last chapter. Take a look at the following script:

Example2

```
using System;
using System.Collections.Generic;
using System.Linq;
using System.Text;
using System.Threading.Tasks;


namespace MyProgram
{
    class Program
    {
        static void Main(string[] args)
        {
            // Creating Object of the
CommercialPlane Class
```

```
            CommercialPlane plane1 = new
CommercialPlane("Airbus", "A350", 400);


            // Creating Object of the
CommercialPlane Class
            FighterPlane plane2 = new
FighterPlane("Lockhead Martin", "F-16", 50);


            // Accessing child class methods
from plane1 object
            plane1.BoardPassenger();


            // Accessing overloaded child
class methods from plane1 object
            plane1.BoardPassenger("business");



            // Accessing child class methods
from plane2 object
            plane2.FireMissile();


            // Accessing overloaded child
class methods from plane2 object
            plane2.FireMissile(false);



            Console.ReadKey();
        }


    }
```

```csharp
class AirPlane
{
    public string planeMake;
    public string planeModel;

    public AirPlane(string make, string
model)
    {
        planeMake = make;
        planeModel = model;
    }

    public void StartPlane()
    {
        Console.WriteLine("Plane
Started");
    }

    public void StopPlane()
    {
        Console.WriteLine("Plane
Stopped");
    }
}

class CommercialPlane : AirPlane
{
    public int passengerCapacity;
```

```csharp
        public CommercialPlane(string make,
string model, int passengerCapacity) :
base(make, model)
        {
            this.passengerCapacity =
passengerCapacity;
        }


        public void BoardPassenger()
        {
            Console.WriteLine("Boarding
Started");
        }


        public void BoardPassenger(string
business)
        {
            Console.WriteLine("Boarding
Started for Business Class");
        }
    }


    class FighterPlane : AirPlane
    {
        public int totalMissiles;


        public FighterPlane(string make,
string model, int totalmissile) : base(make,
model)
        {
            this.totalMissiles = totalmissile;
        }
```

153

```
        public void FireMissile()
        {
            Console.WriteLine("Missile
Fired");
        }


        public void FireMissile(bool bullets)
        {
            Console.WriteLine("Bullets
fired");
        }

    }
}
```

In the script above, we have parent class "AirPlane" and children classes "CommercialPlane" and "FighterPlane". In the "CommercialPlane" class, we have a method named BoardPassenger with no parameter and void return type. We also have its overloaded sibling which accepts one parameter of type string.

Similarly, in the "FighterPlane" class, we have an overloaded "FireMissile" function and its overloaded version that accepts one parameter of type bool.

In the Main method we create objects of both the "CommercialPlane" and "FighterPlane" classes. We then use plane1, which is object of "CommercialPlane" class to call the original and the overloaded

"BoardPassenger" method. In the output, you will see that depending upon the function call, the method with our without parameter will be executed.

Similarly, for FireMissile method of the "FighterPlane" class, if the FireMissile method is called without a parameter, "Missile Fired" will be displayed. However, if the "FireMissile" method is called with a Boolean parameter, "Bullets fired" will be displayed. In short, depending upon the parameters, one function behaves in multiple ways. The output of the script above looks like this:

```
■ C:\Users\Admin\source\repos\MyProgram\MyProgram\bin\
Boarding Started
Boarding Started for Business Class
Missile Fired
Bullets fired
```

Polymorphism via Method Overriding

Another way to implement polymorphism in C# is via method overriding. This type of polymorphism is also known as dynamic polymorphism. Before we actually see dynamic polymorphism in action, let's first study method overriding.

Method Overriding

Method overriding refers to overriding the definition of a method in the parent's class by providing a different definition in the child class. It is important to note that a method has to be declared virtual in the parent class in order for it to be overridden in the child class. To declare a method as virtual, the keyword **virtual** is used. In the child class, the keyword **override** is used to override the virtual method.

Take a look at a simple example of method overriding.

```csharp
using System;
using System.Collections.Generic;
using System.Linq;
using System.Text;
using System.Threading.Tasks;

namespace MyProgram
{
    class Program
    {
        static void Main(string[] args)

        {

            Y y = new Y();
            y.MethodA();

            X x = new X();
            x.MethodA();
```

```
            Console.ReadKey();

        }


    }


    class Y
    {
        public virtual void MethodA()
        {
            Console.WriteLine("This is a
virtual method in the parent class");
        }
    }


    class X:Y
    {
        public override void MethodA()
        {
            Console.WriteLine("This is an
overriden method in the child class");
        }
    }
}
```

In the script above, we have two classes Y and X. The class X inherits the class Y. In the class Y we have a virtual method called MethodA and inside class X we also have a MethodA which overrides the parent class method. In the Main method of the Program class, we create objects of parent class Y and child class X. Now, if you call the MethodA from the object of the child class X, you will see that the overridden method will be executed. However, if you call the MethodA using the object of class Y, you will see that the parent class Y's MethodA will be executed. The output of the script above looks like this:

```
C:\Users\Admin\source\repos\MyProgram\MyProgram\bin'
This is a virtual method in the parent class
This is a virtual method in the parent class
```

Storing Child Class Object in Parent Class Reference

Before we can actually see Polymorphism in action, it is important to understand that an object of child class can be stored in Parent class variable or reference. Take a look at the following script:

```csharp
using System;
using System.Collections.Generic;
using System.Linq;
using System.Text;
using System.Threading.Tasks;


namespace MyProgram
{
    class Program
```

```csharp
{
    static void Main(string[] args)

    {

        Y y = new Y();
        y.MethodA();

        Y x = new X();
        y.MethodA();

        Console.ReadKey();
    }

}

class Y
{
    public virtual void MethodA()
    {
        Console.WriteLine("This is a
virtual method in the parent class");
    }
}

class X:Y
{
    public override void MethodA()
    {
```

```
        Console.WriteLine("This is an
overriden method in the child class");
        }

    }
}
```

The script above is a slight modification of the previous
example. Here in the Main method of the Program
class, you can see that the object reference x is actually
of type Y which is the parent class of X. However the
object of class X is being stored in the reference of class
Y. This shows that child class object can be stored in the
parent class reference.

Polymorphism by Overriding: An Example

Now we know how method overriding works and how
to store a child class object in parent class reference.
Now is the time to see polymorphism in action. Look at
the following example:

```
using System;
using System.Collections.Generic;
using System.Linq;
using System.Text;
using System.Threading.Tasks;


namespace MyProgram
```

```
{
    class Program
    {
        static void Main(string[] args)

        {

            // Creating Object of AirPlane
classs

            // Creating Object of the
CommercialPlane Class
            AirPlane plane1 = new
AirPlane("Airbus", "A350");
            plane1.StartPlane();
            plane1.StopPlane();


            // Creating Object of the
CommercialPlane Class
            AirPlane plane2 = new
CommercialPlane("Airbus", "A350", 400);
            plane2.StartPlane();
            plane2.StopPlane();


            // Creating Object of the
CommercialPlane Class
            AirPlane plane3 = new
FighterPlane("Lockhead Martin", "F-16", 50);
            plane3.StartPlane();
            plane3.StopPlane();
```

```csharp
            Console.ReadKey();
        }

    }

    class AirPlane
    {
        public string planeMake;
        public string planeModel;

        public AirPlane(string make, string
model)
        {
            planeMake = make;
            planeModel = model;
        }

        public virtual void StartPlane()
        {
            Console.WriteLine("Plane
Started");
        }

        public virtual void StopPlane()
        {
            Console.WriteLine("Plane
Stopped");
        }
    }
```

```csharp
class CommercialPlane : AirPlane
{
    public int passengerCapacity;

    public CommercialPlane(string make,
string model, int passengerCapacity) :
base(make, model)
    {
        this.passengerCapacity =
passengerCapacity;
    }

    public override void StartPlane()
    {
        Console.WriteLine("Commercial
Plane Started");
    }

    public override void StopPlane()
    {
        Console.WriteLine("Commercial
Plane Stopped");
    }

    public void BoardPassenger()
    {
        Console.WriteLine("Boarding
Started");
    }
```

```csharp
        }


    class FighterPlane : AirPlane
    {
        public int totalMissiles;

        public FighterPlane(string make,
string model, int totalmissile) : base(make,
model)
        {
            this.totalMissiles = totalmissile;
        }

        public override void StartPlane()
        {
            Console.WriteLine("Fighter Plane
Started");
        }


        public override void StopPlane()
        {
            Console.WriteLine("Fighter Plane
Stopped");
        }

        public void FireMissile()
        {
            Console.WriteLine("Missile
Fired");
        }
```

```
    }
}
```

In the script above we have a parent "AirPlane" class and two children classes "CommercialPlane" and "FighterPlane". The parent class has two virtual methods StartPlane and StopPlane. Inside the children classes, the virtual methods of the parent class have been overridden. In the Main method of the Program class, the objects of the parent, as well as both the child classes have been stored in three parent class references plane1, plane2 and plane3 respectively.

Now, if we call the StartPlane and StopPlane methods from the parent class references plane1, plane2 and plane3, you will see that the StartPlane and StopPlane methods of the corresponding objects will be called. For instance, in the reference plane1, the object of the "AirPlane" class is stored, therefore the StartPlane and StopPlane methods of the "AirPlane" class will be called from the plane1 reference. Similarly, in the parent class reference plane2, the object of the "CommercialPlane" class is stored, therefore the StartPlane and StopPlane methods of the "CommercialPlane" class will be called from the plane2 reference.

The output of the script above looks like this:

```
Plane Started
Plane Stopped
Commercial Plane Started
Commercial Plane Stopped
Fighter Plane Started
Fighter Plane Stopped
```

Encapsulation in Python

In simple words, encapsulation refers to hiding the internal class data. As a rule of thumb, in object oriented programming, class data should not be directly accessible outside the class. Rather, a mechanism should be implemented that ensures secure access to the data. There are different ways to implement encapsulation in Python. In this chapter, we will study two of them.

Encapsulation via Customized Methods

One of the ways to implement encapsulation is by implementing customized methods that can be used to retrieve and set values for the class variables. Take a look at the following example to see how customized methods can be used for implementing encapsulation in C#.

```
using System;
using System.Collections.Generic;
using System.Linq;
using System.Text;
```

```csharp
using System.Threading.Tasks;

namespace MyProgram
{
    class Program
    {
        static void Main(string[] args)

        {
            Y y = new Y();
            y.seta("abc");
            y.setb("xyz");

            Console.WriteLine(y.geta());
            Console.WriteLine(y.getb());
        }
    }

    class Y
    {
        private string a;
        private string b;

        public string geta()
        {
            return a;
        }

        public void seta(string a)
```

```
        {
            this.a = a;
        }


    public string getb()
        {
            return b;
        }


    public void setb(string b)
        {
            this.b = b;
        }


    }

}
```

In the example above, you can see that class Y has two member variables a and b and four methods geta(), getb() and seta(), and setb(). The geta() and getb() methods are used to retrieve the values of a and b variables, respectively. While the seta() and setb() methods are used to set the values of a and b variables respectively.

Encapsulation via Properties

Another way to implement encapsulation is via properties, which contain setters and getters by default. Take a look at the following example to see properties in action:

```
using System;
using System.Collections.Generic;
using System.Linq;
using System.Text;
using System.Threading.Tasks;


namespace MyProgram
{
    class Program
    {
        static void Main(string[] args)

        {
            Y y = new Y();
            y.A = "abc";
            y.B = "xyz";

            Console.WriteLine(y.A);
            Console.WriteLine(y.B);

            Console.ReadKey();
        }
    }
```

```
class Y
{
    private string a;
    private string b;

    public string A
    {
        get
        {
            return this.a;
        }
        set
        {
            this.a = value;
        }
    }

    public string B
    {
        get
        {
            return this.b;
        }
        set
        {
            this.b = value;
        }
    }
```

```
        }

    }
}
```

The output of the script above looks like this:

■ C:\Users\Admin\sour

```
abc
xyz
```

Conclusion

Polymorphism and encapsulation are two of the founding pillars of object oriented programming with Inheritance being the third. We studied Inheritance in the last chapter, In this chapter we studied polymorphism and encapsulation. We studied the different types of polymorphism with the help of examples. Finally we discussed how encapsulation can be implemented in C#. With this we completed our discussion about object oriented programming. In the next chapter, we will see how errors and exceptions are handled in C#.

Chapter 12 – Exception Handling in C#

Exceptions in C# are errors that stop the execution of a program. There are different types of exceptions for instance: divide by zero exceptions, which occurs when an integer is divided by a zero. Other type of exceptions include index out of bound exception which occurs when you try to access array index which doesn't actually exist. The exception handling is the mechanism of avoiding exceptions and preventing computer program from crashing. In this chapter, we will study C# exception handling in detail.

Before we see how exceptions occur and handled, let's first make it clear that all the errors that occur in a program are not exceptions. There are two types of errors that may occur in C# program: Compile time errors and run time errors. Run time errors are called exceptions.

Let's briefly review compile time errors before we move to run time error handling or exceptions.

Compile Time Errors

Compile time errors are the errors which are caught when you compile the program. For instance, if you forget to add a semi-colon at the end of a C# statement, a compile time error will occur telling you that a semi colon is missing. Similarly, if you try to use a function without first importing its namespace, compiler will through an error. The following example demonstrates compile time errors.

```
using System;
using System.Collections.Generic;
using System.Linq;
using System.Text;
using System.Threading.Tasks;

namespace MyProgram
{
    class Program
    {
        static void Main(string[] args)

        {
            Console.WriteLine("abcd")
            WriteCSV("myfile.csv");

            Console.ReadKey();
        }
    }
```

```
}
```

In the above example, there are two errors.

In the line:

```
Console.WriteLine("abcd")
```

There is no semicolon at the end. And in the line:

```
WriteCSV("myfile.csv");
```

The WriteCSV function doesn't exist and we did not import any namespace that contains this function.

When you try to run the above code via Visual Studio, you will see the following errors:

You can clearly see that both the errors in the program have been caught before the program runs. Compile time errors are less threatening when compared to run time errors or exceptions, since the former can be caught before the program executes. Runtime errors or exceptions are extremely dangerous since they are not caught unless the program actually runs.

Runtime Errors (Exceptions)

Exceptions occur at runtime. If during the execution of a program an unexpected event occurs which cannot be handled by a system, an exception is thrown. For instance, if you try to read a file which doesn't actually exist, an exception will occur. Such an error cannot be caught at compile time since nobody knows at compile time whether or not the file exists. Let's see such exception or run time errors in action. Execute the following script:

```csharp
using System;
using System.Collections.Generic;
using System.IO;
using System.Linq;
using System.Text;
using System.Threading.Tasks;

namespace MyProgram
{
    class Program
    {
        static void Main(string[] args)

        {
            TextReader reader = new StreamReader("abc.txt");

            Console.ReadKey();
        }
    }
```

```
}
```

In the script above the StreamReader is used to read the file "abc.txt" which actually doesn't exit. Therefore, when the above program is run, an exception is thrown as shown below:

The name of the exception i.e. "FileNotFoundException" is self-explanatory.

How Exceptions are handled

To understand exception handling, it is pertinent to understand the concept of call stack. As explained earlier, a C# program starts from the Main method. Inside the Main method we may call Method1 which in turn calls Method2 and so on up to MethodN. The method that are called later are placed on the stack and when the method execution completes, the methods are pulled out of the stack. Now If an exception occurs in MethodN, the C#'s runtime looks for exception handler in MethodN, if it doesn't find exception handler in MethodN, it looks for the handler on the next method down the method call stack. It keeps looking for handler in the subsequent methods down the stack unless the Main method is reached. If handler is found in any of the methods, the code for the handler executes, else the application crashes.

Let's see exception handling in Action.

```
using System;
using System.Collections.Generic;
using System.IO;
using System.Linq;
using System.Text;
using System.Threading.Tasks;


namespace MyProgram
{
    class Program
    {
        static void Main(string[] args)


        {


            try
            {
                Method1();
            }
            catch (Exception e)
            {
```

```
            Console.WriteLine(e.Message);
        }


        Console.ReadKey();
    }


    public static void Method1()
    {
        TextReader reader = new
StreamReader("abc.txt");
    }

}
}
```

The Try Block

To implement exception handling, the code which is likely to throw exception is surrounded with a try block. The try block can be created using **try** keyword. In the script above, we know that Method1() can throw an exception, therefore we surrounded the call to Method1() in try block.

The Catch Block

The catch block contains the exception handling code. The catch block must immediately follow the try block. The catch block is created using the **catch** keyword. The exception is thrown in the form of exception object, the base class of which is Exception. In the catch block, you can catch the exception and print the exception detail on the console. In the script above, the file not found exception will occur as shown below:

The Finally Block

The finally block follows the try or catch block (if any) and executes irrespective of the exception. The finally block is normally used to relieve the resources occupied by the objects that threw exception. Let's modify the last example to see the working of finally block. Execute the following script:

```
using System;
using System.Collections.Generic;
using System.IO;
using System.Linq;
using System.Text;
using System.Threading.Tasks;

namespace MyProgram
{
    class Program
    {
        static void Main(string[] args)
        {
            {
```

```
            try
            {
                Method1();
            }
            catch (Exception e)
            {
                Console.WriteLine(e.Message);
            }
            finally
            {
                Console.WriteLine("Try block
executed");
            }

            Console.ReadKey();
        }

        public static void Method1()
        {
            TextReader reader = new
StreamReader("abc.txt");
        }
    }
}
```

The output of the script above looks like this:

```
Could not find file 'C:\Users\Admin\source\repos\MyProgram\MyProgram\bin\Debug\abc.txt'.
Try block executed
```

In the example above, you would have noticed that the code that raises the exception is actually in Method1 where the file is being read, however the exception is being caught in the Main method. This is because of the fact that there is no try and catch block in the Method1 itself.

Let's modify the previous example to add try and catch block inside Method1 and see how the exception is handled. Take a look at the following script:

```csharp
using System;
using System.Collections.Generic;
using System.IO;
using System.Linq;
using System.Text;
using System.Threading.Tasks;

namespace MyProgram
{
    class Program
    {
        static void Main(string[] args)

        {

            Method1();
```

181

```
                Console.ReadKey();
        }


        public static void Method1()
        {
            try
            {
                TextReader reader = new
StreamReader("abc.txt");
            }
            catch (Exception e)
            {
                Console.WriteLine(e.Message);
            }
            finally
            {
                Console.WriteLine("Try block
executed inside Method1");
            }
        }
    }
}
```

The output of the script above looks like this:

C:\Users\Admin\source\repos\MyProgram\MyProgram\bin\Debug\MyProgram.exe

```
Could not find file 'C:\Users\Admin\source\repos\MyProgram\MyProgra
Try block executed inside Method1
```

You can clearly see that the exception is being handled in the catch block of the Method1.

Conclusion

Handling exceptions and errors is crucial to the seamless and successful execution of a program. In this chapter, we saw what C# exceptions are, what their different types are and how they can be handled using try, catch and finally blocks. In the next chapter, we will start our discussion about string handling in C#.

Chapter 13 – String Manipulation in C#

A string is one of the most important data type in any programming language. While integers and decimals are useful for performing arithmetic operations, strings are extremely useful for getting information from the user and displaying information to the user. It is for this reason that we have dedicated a full chapter to string manipulation in C#.

In this chapter, we will see the basics of C# strings along with how they are created and what are some of the most commonly used string function.

Creating a String

A string is basically a sequence of characters. In C#, strings are instances of **System.String** class. However, we can simply declare a string using keyword **string** which is an alias for **System.String.**

There are two main ways of creating a string. You can create a string literal and store it in a string type variable as shown below:

```
static void Main(string[] args)


    {
            string color = "red";
            Console.WriteLine(color);
            Console.ReadKey();

    }
```

In the output, you should see string "red" displayed in the console window. It is important to mention here that string is the only object that can be created without the **new** keyword. In the above script, when you create an object literal "red", it basically creates a string type object and stores it in the "color" variable.

There is a way to create a string object using the **new** keyword. Take a look at the following example:

```
static void Main(string[] args)


        {
            char[] col = new char[] { 'b',
'l', 'u', 'e' };

            string color = new string(col);
            Console.WriteLine(color);

            Console.ReadKey();

        }
```

185

In the script above, we create a character array "col". We then use keyword **new** to call the constructor of the string class and pass it the character type array and in return, we get a string of all the characters in the character array. If you execute the script above, you will see "blue" printed on the console.

Just to confirm that a string is actually an array of characters, let's use the **for each** loop to iterate through string characters. Take a look at the following script:

```
static void Main(string[] args)

    {

        string message = "C# is awesome";
        foreach(char c in message)
        {
            Console.WriteLine(c);
        }

        Console.ReadKey();
    }
```

In the output, you should see characters of the string displayed on a separate line as shown below:

Using Single and Double Quotes

To use single and double quotes, you need to put a backward slash before single and double quotes. Take a look at the following example:

```
static void Main(string[] args)
        {
        string message = "This is Jame\'s
\"Car\"";

        Console.WriteLine(message);
        Console.ReadKey();
```

187

```
        }
```

Output:

C:\Users\Admin\source\repos\

This is Jame's "Car"

String Concatenation

String concatenation refers to joining two or more than two strings. In C#, there are two ways to join strings. You can use the concatenation operator "+", the "Join()" and the "Concat()" methods. The following example demonstrates string concatenation in action:

```
static void Main(string[] args)
        {
            string message1 = "Welcome to";
            string message2 = " C#";

            string result1 = message1 +
message2;

            string result2 = string.Join(" ",
message1, message2);
```

```
            string result3 =
string.Concat(message1, message2);

            Console.WriteLine(result1);
            Console.WriteLine(result2);
            Console.WriteLine(result3);

            Console.ReadKey();
        }
```

In the script above, we have two strings message1 and
message2. In the first instance, we use the plus
operator to concatenate the two strings. Next, we use
the Join() function to concatenate the strings. It is
important to mention that the first parameter to the
join function is actually the string which is used as a
separator between the two strings. The rest of the
parameters are the strings to be concatenated. Finally,
the Concat() method also takes the string to join as
parameters and return a concatenated string. The
output of the script above looks like this:

C:\Users\Admin\source\repos\MyProgram\M'
Welcome to C#
Welcome to C#
Welcome to C#

Converting String to Lowercase and Uppercase

Converting a string into uppercase or lower case is another fundamental task in string manipulation. Luckily, C# comes with ToUpper() and ToLower() methods that can be used to convert a string to upper or lowercase respectively. Take a look at the following example:

```
static void Main(string[] args)
        {
            string message1 = "HELLO TO C#";
            string message2 = "it is the best
language";


Console.WriteLine(message1.ToLower());

Console.WriteLine(message2.ToUpper());

            Console.ReadKey();
        }
```

In the script above we have an all uppercase string in message1 and an all lowercase string in message2. However, when we display these strings on the console, we convert the uppercase string to lowercase using the ToLower() method. Similarly, the all-lowercase string is converted to an uppercase string using the ToUpper() method. The output of the script above looks like this:

```
C:\Users\Admin\source\repos\MyProgram\M
hello to c#
IT IS THE BEST LANGUAGE
```

Finding Substring

A substring is a string within another string. C# has a variety of methods that can be used to find the occurrence of a string within another string, extracting a string, finding the index of a string and so on. In this section, we will see some of the substring methods.

To see if a string exists inside another string, we can use IndexOf() method as follows. Take a look at the following example:

```
static void Main(string[] args)
        {
            string message1 = "HELLO TO C#";
            int index1 =
message1.IndexOf("C#");
```

```
        int index2 =
message1.IndexOf("Java");

        Console.WriteLine(index1);
        Console.WriteLine(index2);

        Console.ReadKey();
    }
```

In the script above we have a string "HELLO TO C#". We use the IndexOf() method to first check if the string contains "C#". If the string is found, the IndexOff() method returns the index of the starting position of the string being searched. The starting position of the string "C#" in the string "HELLO TO C#" is 9. Next, we again use the IndexOf() method to search for the string "Java", however since the string "HELLO TO C#" doesn't contain a substring "Java", the IndexOf() method will return -1 which means that the string was not found.

To extract a piece of string from another string, you can use the Substring() method. The method takes the starting index of the string to extract as the first parameter. The second parameter is the number of characters to extract. If you do not specify the second parameter, the string will be extracted from the index passed by the first parameter to the end of the string. Take a look at the following example:

```
static void Main(string[] args)
        {
            string message1 = "HELLO TO C#";
            string sub = message1.Substring(9,
2);

            Console.WriteLine(sub);

            Console.ReadKey();
        }
```

In the script above, we are extracting 2 characters starting from 9th index from the string "HELLO TO C#". We know that C is at index 9 and extracting two characters from there would return the string "C#".

Splitting Strings

You can split strings by calling Split() function on the string. The Split() function takes separator as an argument. You can pass multiple separators to the Split() method in the form of an array. Take a look at the following script to see string splitting in action.

```
    static void Main(string[] args)
    {
        string message1 = "HELLO TO C#";
        string [] split1 =
message1.Split(' ');

        string[] split2 =
message1.Split(new char[] { 'T', 'E' });

        foreach (string s in split1)
        {
            Console.WriteLine(s);
        }


Console.WriteLine("=============================
===========");

        foreach (string s in split2)
        {
            Console.WriteLine(s);
        }

        Console.ReadKey();
    }
```

In the script above we split the string "Hello to C#" twice. First, we split the string by a single space. Next, we use a char array of two characters "T" and "E" and use this array to split the string. It is important to mention that the Split() method returns an array of strings that are split as a result of the Split() function. In the script above, we iterate through the arrays of the string returned by the Split() function. The output of the script above looks like this:

```
C:\Users\Admin\source\repos\MyProgram\MyProgram\bin\Debu
HELLO
TO
C#
--------------------------------------------------------
H
LLO
O C#
```

You can see that since the first string was split using space, we have individual words in the output array. However, the second string was split using the characters T and E, we have incomplete words in the output.

Replacing a String

A substring can be replaced by another string using the Replace() method. The first parameter to the replace() method is the string that you want to be replaced and the second parameter is the new string which you want to append in place of the string passed as the first parameter. Take a look at the following script:

```
static void Main(string[] args)
```

195

```
        {
            string message1 = "HELLO TO C#";
            string message2 =
message1.Replace("C#", "JAVA");

            Console.WriteLine(message2);
            Console.ReadKey();
        }
```

In the script above, we use the Replace() function to replace "C#" in the string "HELLO TO C#" with the "JAVA". In the output, you should see the replaced text as shown below:

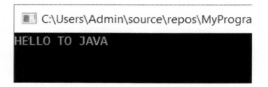

Finding String Length

Length of a string is equal to a number of characters in a string including empty spaces. To find the length of a string in C#, you can either use the "length" attribute of string object or you can use Count() function. The following script explains both the ways:

```
static void Main(string[] args)
        {
```

```
string message1 = "HELLO TO C#";
int length1 = message1.Length;

int length2 = message1.Count();

Console.WriteLine(length1);
Console.WriteLine(length2);
Console.ReadKey();
}
```

In the script above, we first use the "length" attribute to find the length or size of the string. Next we use the Count() function to find the same. In the output, you will see 11 since there are 11 characters in the string "HELLO TO C#".

Conclusion

String manipulation is one of the most crucial tasks, particular for applications that involve user interactivity. In this chapter, we studied string manipulation in detail. We studied how strings can be defined along with some of the most commonly used string operations. In the next chapter, we will study how files are handled in C#.

Chapter 14 – File Handling in C#

Writing data to a file and reading data from a file are some of the most fundamental tasks of a computer application. To keep data persistent, we need to write data to file which can be read later. Though databases are mostly used for storing persistent data, the important of flat files can still not be ignored, particularly if you want to store unstructured, unrelated data. In this section, we will see how file handling can be performed using C#. We will various ways in which files can be accessed, read, written and updated.

Reading a File

Though there are several ways to read and write data to a file, the easiest way is to make use of the *File* class of the System.IO library. The *File* class comes with a variety of functionalities to perform different file-related tasks such as creating a new file, reading data from a file, writing and appending data to a file, deleting a file and so on.

In this section, we will see how the *File* class can be used for reading a file. Before you execute the following script, create a file named "mytext.txt" and place it in the "D" directory. The contents of the text file should look like this:

```
Hello C# is awesome
You can develop web applications
as well as desktop applications
with it
```

ReadAllText()

To read the data from "myfile.txt", we will use the ReadAllText() method of the *File* class. Take a look at the following script:

```csharp
using System;
using System.Collections.Generic;
using System.IO;
using System.Linq;
using System.Text;
using System.Threading.Tasks;


namespace MyProgram
{

    class Program
    {

        static void Main(string[] args)
```

```
        {
            if (File.Exists("D:/myfile.txt"))
            {
                string text =
File.ReadAllText("D:/myfile.txt");
                Console.WriteLine("The file
has following content");
                Console.WriteLine(text);
            }

            Console.ReadLine();
        }

    }
}
```

In the script above, we first use the Exist() method of
the *File* class to see if "myfile.txt" actually exists. If the
file exists, we then use the ReadAllText() method of the
File class and pass it the file path. The ReadAllText()
method returns a multiline string that contains the text
of the fie. Finally, we print the text on the console. The
output of the script above looks like this:

```
■ C:\Users\Admin\source\repos\MyProgram\M
The file has following content
Hello C# is awesome
You can develop web applications
as well as desktop applications
with it
```

ReadAllLines()

Another way to read the contents of a file is by using ReadAllLines() method which returns an array of string where each string corresponds to one line in the text file. Take a look at the following script:

```csharp
using System.Linq;
using System.Text;
using System.Threading.Tasks;

namespace MyProgram
{
    class Program
    {
        static void Main(string[] args)
        {
            if (File.Exists("D:/myfile.txt"))
            {
```

201

```
                string [] text =
File.ReadAllLines("D:/myfile.txt");

                Console.WriteLine("The file
has following content");


                foreach(string line in text)

                {

                        Console.WriteLine(line);

                }


        }


        Console.ReadLine();

    }

  }

}
```

In the script above, we again first check if the file exists
or not. If the file exists we use the ReadAllLines()
method of the *File* class to read the contents of the file
The method takes file path as parameter and returns an
array of string. Next, we use the *foreach* loop to iterate
through all the lines in the text file. The output will look
like:

```
The file has following content
Hello C# is awesome
You can develop web applications
as well as desktop applications
with it
```

ReadLines()

In addition to ReadAllText() and ReadAllLines(), the **File** class also contains a method ReadLines() which reads the content of the file line by line. The ReadLines() method should be preferred if the text file has a large number of data since ReadLines() method returns the line as soon as it reads it. On the other hand, the ReadAllLines() method first read all the lines from the text file and then return an array of all lines at once to the user. The return type of ReadLines() method is IEnumerable<string>. Take a look at the following script top see ReadLines() function in action.

```csharp
using System;
using System.Collections.Generic;
using System.IO;
using System.Linq;
using System.Text;
using System.Threading.Tasks;
```

```
namespace MyProgram
{

    class Program
    {

        static void Main(string[] args)
        {

            if (File.Exists("D:/myfile.txt"))
            {


                foreach(string line in
File.ReadLines("D:/myfile.txt"))
                {

                    Console.WriteLine(line);

                }


            }


            Console.ReadLine();

        }


    }

}
```

In the script above, you can see that as soon as a line of text is read, it is being displayed on the console using the *foreach* loop.

Writing Data to File

Just as there are multiple ways to read a file, there are several ways to write data to file. In this section, we will see how we can write content to a text file.

WriteAllText()

The main way to write all the content to a text file is via the WriteAllText() method. The method takes two arguments. The first argument is the path of the file that you want your data written to and the second argument is the content that you want to write. Take a look at the following example:

```
using System;
using System.Collections.Generic;
using System.IO;
using System.Linq;
using System.Text;
using System.Threading.Tasks;

namespace MyProgram
{
    class Program
    {
        static void Main(string[] args)
        {
```

```
        Console.WriteLine("Enter the
content you want to write to file:");

        string text = Console.ReadLine();

File.WriteAllText("D:/myfile2.txt", text);


        Console.ReadLine();

    }


  }


}
```

In the script above, we ask the user to enter the content that he wants to write in the file. Next, we use the WriteAllText() method to write the contents entered by the user to the file "myfile.txt". If the "myfile.txt" doesn't already exist, you will see that the WriteAllText() method will automatically create a new file named "myfile.txt" and will write the text to the file. If the file already exists, the existing text will be overwritten. Once you execute the script above, you should see a file named "myfile.txt" containing the content you entered in the console window.

WriteAllLines()

In addition to WriteAllText() which writes all the data to file at once, you can also use the WriteAllLines() method which takes an array of string as the second argument.

In the text file, it creates a new line for each item in the string array. Look at the following script to see WriteAllLines() method in action:

```
using System;
using System.Collections.Generic;
using System.IO;
using System.Linq;
using System.Text;
using System.Threading.Tasks;

namespace MyProgram
{
    class Program
    {
        static void Main(string[] args)
        {

            Console.WriteLine("Enter first
line");
            string text = Console.ReadLine();

            Console.WriteLine("Enter second
line");
            string text2 = Console.ReadLine();


            Console.WriteLine("Enter third
line");
```

```
            string text3 = Console.ReadLine();

            string[] texts = { text, text2,
text3 };


File.WriteAllLines("D:/myfile2.txt", texts);


            Console.ReadLine();

        }


    }

}
```

In the script above, the user is asked thrice to enter any text. The texts are stored in three string type variables. The string type variables are then used to create an array of string which is passed to the WriteAllLines() method. Once you execute the script above, you should see three lines that you entered in the "myfile2.txt" file.

AppendAllText()

Instead of overwriting the already existing text, you can append the text at the end of the file. To do so, you can use the AppendAllText() method. Take a look at the following script:

```csharp
using System;
using System.Collections.Generic;
using System.IO;
using System.Linq;
using System.Text;
using System.Threading.Tasks;

namespace MyProgram
{
    class Program
    {
        static void Main(string[] args)
        {

            Console.WriteLine("Enter the
content you want to write to file:");
            string text = Console.ReadLine();

File.AppendAllText("D:/myfile2.txt", text);

            Console.ReadLine();

        }

    }

}
```

In the script above, the text entered by the user is appended at the end of the already existing text in "myfile2.txt".

AppendAllLines()

Similarly, if you want to append multiple lines to an already existing file, you can use AppendAllLines() method as shown in the following script:

```
using System;
using System.Collections.Generic;
using System.IO;
using System.Linq;
using System.Text;
using System.Threading.Tasks;

namespace MyProgram
{
    class Program
    {
        static void Main(string[] args)
        {

            Console.WriteLine("Enter first
line");

            string text = Console.ReadLine();
```

```
            Console.WriteLine("Enter second
line");

            string text2 = Console.ReadLine();



            Console.WriteLine("Enter third
line");

            string text3 = Console.ReadLine();


            string[] texts = { text, text2,
text3 };


File.AppendAllLines("D:/myfile2.txt", texts);


            Console.ReadLine();

        }


    }


}
```

Once, you execute the script above, you should see three lines that you enter, appended at the end of the "myfile2.txt" file.

Creating a File

As discussed earlier, the **File** class can be used to create a file of any type. The following script, when executed creates a file "content.pdf" in the root of the "D" directory.

211

```
using System;
using System.Collections.Generic;
using System.IO;
using System.Linq;
using System.Text;
using System.Threading.Tasks;

namespace MyProgram
{
    class Program
    {
        static void Main(string[] args)
        {

            File.Create("D:/Content.pdf");
            Console.WriteLine("New File
Created");

            Console.ReadLine();
        }

    }
}
```

Deleting a File

Similarly, you can delete a file using the Delete()
method of the *File* class as shown below:

```
using System;
using System.Collections.Generic;
using System.IO;
using System.Linq;
using System.Text;
using System.Threading.Tasks;

namespace MyProgram
{

    class Program
    {

        static void Main(string[] args)
        {

            File.Delete("D:/Content.pdf");
            Console.WriteLine("File deleted");

            Console.ReadLine();
        }

    }

}
```

213

The above script will delete the "Content.pdf" file from the root directory of the "D" drive.

Conclusion

File handling refers to creating, deleting, reading and writing of files using a computer program and is one of the most important tasks in application development. In this chapter, we studied how we can create, delete and modfy files. We also studied how to read text files, how to write data to a text file and how to append data to text files. In the next chapter, we will start our discussion about collections in C#.

Chapter 15 – Collections in C#

In a previous chapter, we studied arrays in detail. We know that arrays are used to store a collection of data in contagious memory locations. In addition to arrays, C# contains more specialized collections that are used to store data in a specific format. C# collections come in two formats: Generic Collections and Non-Generic collections. The name collection is by default used for non-generic collections. On the other hand, generic collections are simply called generics. In this chapter, we will study non-generic collections or simply known as collections.

What are Collections?

Collections are special data structures that store data in a specific format. The collections are stored in **System.Collections** namespace. All the collection classes inherit **IEnumerator**, **IEnumerable** and **ICollection** interfaces. The **IEnumerator** interface allows iteration over items in the collections The **IEnumerable** interface is used to return the next item in the collection and the **ICollections** interface define general collection functions such as size definition etc.

Following are the most commonly used classes in the *System.Collections* namespace:

- ## ArrayList:

An ArrayList collection is similar to the basic C# array. However, in case of ArrayList, you don't have to specify the size of the ArrayList.

- ## SortedList

SortedList stores item in the form of key and value pairs and by default sorts the item in ascending order of the keys.

- ## Stack

A Stock follows principle of LIFO(Last in, First Out). The item inserted last will be removed first. The Stack has a method Push() which pushes the item on top of the stack. Similarly, it has a method Pop() which removes the data from the top of the stack.

- ## Queue

A queue follows the principle of FIFO where the item inserted first is removed first.

In this chapter, we will see these collections in detail.

ArrayList

Creating an ArrayList

To create an ArrayList, you can use the **new** keyword like any other class. Take a look at the following script:

```
using System;
using System.Collections.Generic;
using System.IO;
using System.Linq;
using System.Text;
using System.Threading.Tasks;
using System.Collections;

namespace MyProgram
{
    class Program
    {
        static void Main(string[] args)
        {

            ArrayList items = new ArrayList();

            Console.ReadLine();
        }

    }
```

```
}
```

In the above script, we simply create an ArrayList item. It is important to mention, that you need to import the namespace "System.Collections" namespace before you can use ArrayList or for that matter, any other collection.

Adding Elements to an ArrayList

You can use Add(), AddRange() and Insert() methods to add elements to an ArrayList. The Add() and AddRange() methods add the elements at the end, while the Insert() method inserts the element at the specified index. Look at the following example:

```
using System;
using System.Collections.Generic;
using System.IO;
using System.Linq;
using System.Text;
using System.Threading.Tasks;
using System.Collections;

namespace MyProgram
{
    class Program
```

```csharp
{
    static void Main(string[] args)
    {

        ArrayList items = new ArrayList();

        items.Add("abc");
        items.Add(13);
        items.Add(true);

        IList nums = new ArrayList()
        {
            10, 20, 30
        };
        items.AddRange(nums);

        items.Insert(2, "False");

        foreach(var item in items)
        {
            Console.WriteLine(item);
        }

        Console.ReadLine();
    }
}
}
```

In the script above, we create an ArrayList "items " and add a string, an integer, and a Boolean value into it. We then use AddRange() method to add three integers. Finally, we used Insert() method to insert a Boolean value "False" at the second index. Next, a "foreach" loop has is used to iterate through the ArrayList. The output of the script above looks like this:

C:\Users\Admin\source\repos\MyProgram\MyProgram\bin\D

```
abc
13
False
True
10
20
30
```

In addition to AddRange(), you can also use InsertRange() function to add a range of elements to an array. The first parameter is the index where you want to insert the range and the second parameter is the list of elements to be added.

Removing Elements from an ArrayList

To remove an element from an ArrayList, you could use both Remove() and RemoveAt() functions. The Remove() function requires the element to be removed, on the other hand the RemoveAt() function takes the index of the element to be removed. Take a look at the following example:

220

```csharp
using System;
using System.Collections.Generic;
using System.IO;
using System.Linq;
using System.Text;
using System.Threading.Tasks;
using System.Collections;

namespace MyProgram
{
    class Program
    {
        static void Main(string[] args)
        {

            ArrayList items = new ArrayList();

            items.Add("abc");
            items.Add(13);
            items.Add(true);

            IList nums = new ArrayList()
            {
                10, 20, 30
            };
            items.AddRange(nums);
```

221

```
            items.Insert(2, "False");

        foreach(var item in items)
        {
            Console.WriteLine(item);
        }

        items.Remove(13);
        items.RemoveAt(2);

        Console.WriteLine("After removing
words ...");

        foreach (var item in items)
        {
            Console.WriteLine(item);
        }
        Console.ReadLine();
    }

}

}
```

In the script above, we added some items in the
ArrayList named items. We then removed the item "13"
and the item at index 2. Once, you print the items
ArrayList, after removing the elements, you will not see

222

item 13 and "true" which was at index 2. The output of the above script looks like this:

Accessing Elements from an ArrayList

ArrayList elements can be accessed easily with the help of their index number. However, since an ArrayList can have elements of multiple types, you will need to first cast the element to its corresponding type.

For instance, take a look at the following example:

```
using System;
using System.Collections.Generic;
using System.IO;
using System.Linq;
using System.Text;
using System.Threading.Tasks;
using System.Collections;

namespace MyProgram
{
    class Program
    {
        static void Main(string[] args)
        {
```

```csharp
            ArrayList items = new ArrayList();

            items.Add("abc");
            items.Add(13);
            items.Add(true);

            IList nums = new ArrayList()
            {
                10, 20, 30
            };
            items.AddRange(nums);

            items.Insert(2, "False");

            int num1 = (int)items[1];
            Console.WriteLine(num1);

            string alphabet =
(string)(items[0]);
            Console.WriteLine(alphabet);
            Console.ReadLine();
        }

    }

}
```

In the script above, we try to print the first and the second element of the items ArrayList. Notice that the first index has a string, therefore we cast the item into string type before using it. Similarly, the second element is an integer and therefore have been cast into the integer type. The output of the script above looks like this:

Reversing and Sorting an ArrayList

You can use Reverse() and Sort() functions to reverse and sort an array respectively. Look at the following script:

```
using System;
using System.Collections.Generic;
using System.IO;
using System.Linq;
using System.Text;
using System.Threading.Tasks;
using System.Collections;
```

```csharp
namespace MyProgram
{
    class Program
    {
        static void Main(string[] args)
        {

            ArrayList items = new ArrayList();

            items.Add(10);
            items.Add(50);
            items.Add(5);
            items.Add(145);
            items.Add(30);



            items.Reverse();
            Console.WriteLine(" ====== After
reversing =======");
            foreach (var element in items)
            {
                Console.WriteLine(element);
            }


            items.Sort();
            Console.WriteLine("====== After
sorting =======");
```

```
        foreach (var element in items)
        {
            Console.WriteLine(element);
        }

        Console.ReadLine();
    }
}
}
```

In the script above, we create an ArrayList "items" with random integers. We then used the Reverse() method to first reverse the list and then we used the Sort() method to sort the list in ascending order. The output of the script above looks like this:

C:\Users\Admin\source\repos\MyProgram\My

```
======= After reversing =======
30
145
5
50
10
======= After sorting =======
5
10
30
50
145
```

SortedList

As discussed earlier, a SortedList stores data in the form of key values pair. By default, the items are sorted on the basis of keys.

Creating a SortedList

It is straight forward to create a SortedList in C#. You have to use the *new* keyword followed by the class name SortedList() as shown below:

```
using System;
using System.Collections.Generic;
using System.IO;
using System.Linq;
using System.Text;
using System.Threading.Tasks;
using System.Collections;

namespace MyProgram
{
    class Program
    {
        static void Main(string[] args)
        {
```

```
            SortedList slist = new
SortedList();

            Console.ReadLine();
        }

    }

}
```

In the script above, we create a sorted list named "slist". You can also add, items to a sorted list while creating the list itself. Have a look at the script below:

```
using System;
using System.Collections.Generic;
using System.IO;
using System.Linq;
using System.Text;
using System.Threading.Tasks;
using System.Collections;


namespace MyProgram
{
    class Program
    {
        static void Main(string[] args)
```

```
        {

                SortedList slist = new
SortedList() {
                    {2, "Red"},
                    {4, "Blue"},
                    {5, "Green"},
                    {1, "Orange"},
                    {3, "Pink"}
                };


                Console.ReadLine();
        }


    }

}
```

Adding Elements to a SortedList

To add elements to an ArrayList, you can simply use the Add() method. The add method accepts a tuple which consists of a key value pair. Take a look at the following example:

```
using System;
using System.Collections.Generic;
using System.IO;
```

```
using System.Linq;
using System.Text;
using System.Threading.Tasks;
using System.Collections;

namespace MyProgram
{
    class Program
    {
        static void Main(string[] args)
        {

            SortedList slist = new
SortedList();
                slist.Add(2, "Red");
                slist.Add(4, "Blue");
                slist.Add(5, "Green");
                slist.Add(1, "Orange");
                slist.Add(3, "Pink");

            Console.WriteLine(slist.Count);
            Console.ReadLine();

        }

    }

}
```

In the script above, we add five elements to our
SortedList using the Add method. Next, we verify the

number of items in the SortedList using the count function. In the console output, you should see 5 onve you run the script above.

It is important to mention here that though values in a SortedList can be of different data types, the data type of Keys for all the items must remain the same. Take a look at the following example:

```
using System;
using System.Collections.Generic;
using System.IO;
using System.Linq;
using System.Text;
using System.Threading.Tasks;
using System.Collections;

namespace MyProgram
{
    class Program
    {
        static void Main(string[] args)
        {

            SortedList slist = new
SortedList();
            slist.Add(2, "Red");
            slist.Add("three", "Blue");
            slist.Add(5, "Green");
```

```
            slist.Add(1, "Orange");
            slist.Add(3, "Pink");


        Console.WriteLine(slist.Count);
        Console.ReadLine();

    }


}
}
```

In the above script, the data type for the key of the first element in the SortedList is an integer. On the other hand, the data type for the key of the second element is a string. Therefore, when you execute the above script, you will receive the following exception.

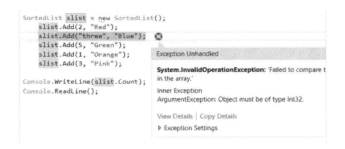

Accessing Elements in a SortedList

There are multiple ways to access items in a SortedList. The simples way is to pass the key as an index to the SortedList as shown below:

```
using System;
using System.Collections.Generic;
using System.IO;
using System.Linq;
using System.Text;
using System.Threading.Tasks;
using System.Collections;


namespace MyProgram
{
    class Program
    {
        static void Main(string[] args)
        {

            SortedList slist = new
SortedList();
                slist.Add(2, "Red");
                slist.Add(4, "Blue");
                slist.Add(5, "Green");
                slist.Add(1, "Orange");
                slist.Add(3, "Pink");

            string item = (string)slist[5];
```

```
                Console.WriteLine(item);


                Console.ReadLine();

        }


    }

}
```

In the above script, we access the element with the key of 5 from the SortedList "slist". The value for the key 5 is "green". Therefore, in the console output, you will see green printed.

To access all the elements in an array, you can make use of a for loop in combination with the GetKey() method and the GetByIndex(i) method. Both these methods take an index as a parameter and return the key and value at the specified index, respectively. Take a look at the following example:

```
using System;
using System.Collections.Generic;
using System.IO;
using System.Linq;
using System.Text;
using System.Threading.Tasks;
using System.Collections;
```

```
namespace MyProgram
{
    class Program
    {
        static void Main(string[] args)
        {

            SortedList slist = new
SortedList();
                slist.Add(2, "Red");
                slist.Add(4, "Blue");
                slist.Add(5, "Green");
                slist.Add(1, "Orange");
                slist.Add(3, "Pink");


            for (int i = 0; i < slist.Count;
i++)
            {
                Console.WriteLine("Key:" +
slist.GetKey(i) + ", Value:" +
slist.GetByIndex(i));
            }


            Console.ReadLine();
        }


    }

}
```

In the script above, we iterate through all the items in the "slist" using a for loop. The output of the script above looks like this:

```
C:\Users\Admin\source\repos\MyProgram\MyProgram\bin\Debug\M
Key:1, Value:Orange
Key:2, Value:Red
Key:3, Value:Pink
Key:4, Value:Blue
Key:5, Value:Green
```

From the output, you can see that the items have been displayed in the ascending order of the key. This is due to the fact that items in the SortedList are by default sorted by the ascending order of the keys.

Removing Elements from SortedList

To remove elements from a SortedList, you can use both Remove() and RemoveAt() functions. The Remove() function takes the key of the element to be removed while the RemoveAt() function takes the index. Look at the following script:

```
using System;
using System.Collections.Generic;
```

```csharp
using System.IO;
using System.Linq;
using System.Text;
using System.Threading.Tasks;
using System.Collections;


namespace MyProgram
{
    class Program
    {
        static void Main(string[] args)
        {

            SortedList slist = new
SortedList();
                slist.Add(2, "Red");
                slist.Add(4, "Blue");
                slist.Add(5, "Green");
                slist.Add(1, "Orange");
                slist.Add(3, "Pink");

            slist.Remove(1);
            slist.RemoveAt(0);


            for (int i = 0; i < slist.Count;
i++)
            {
                Console.WriteLine("Key:" +
slist.GetKey(i) + ", Value:" +
slist.GetByIndex(i));
```

```
            }


        Console.ReadLine();


    }


  }

}
```

In the script above, we first remove the element with key 1. Next, we remove the element at 0th index which is basically the element with key 2, since after removing key 1, the element with key 2 moves to index 0. Finally, we print the remaining elements on the screen. You will see the elements with key 3,4 and 5 will be printed on the screen.

```
C:\Users\Admin\source\repos\MyProgram\MyProgram\bin
Key:3, Value:Pink
Key:4, Value:Blue
Key:5, Value:Green
```

Stack

Stacks follow the principle of LIFO where the elements inserted last are removed first.

Creating a Stack

To create a stack, you can use the ***new*** keyword followed by the name of the class "Stack" as shown below:

```
using System;
using System.Collections.Generic;
using System.IO;
using System.Linq;
using System.Text;
using System.Threading.Tasks;
using System.Collections;

namespace MyProgram
{
    class Program
    {
        static void Main(string[] args)
        {

            Stack newstack = new Stack();

            Console.ReadLine();
        }

    }
```

Adding Elements to a Stack

To add elements to Stack, you can use the Push ()
method which stores elements at the top of a stack as
shown below:

```
using System;
using System.Collections.Generic;
using System.IO;
using System.Linq;
using System.Text;
using System.Threading.Tasks;
using System.Collections;

namespace MyProgram
{
    class Program
    {
        static void Main(string[] args)
        {

            Stack newstack = new Stack();
            newstack.Push(true);
            newstack.Push(20);
            newstack.Push("Hello");
```

```
            newstack.Push(1.56);

        Console.WriteLine(newstack.Count);

        Console.ReadLine();
    }

  }

}
```

In the script above, we add four items to the Stack "mystack". You can see that a Stack can contain items of different data types. Next, we printed the number of items in the stack on the console.

Accessing Elements from a Stack

There are multiple ways to access elements from a Stack. You can use the Peek() method which returns a single item from the top of the stack. Take a look at the following example.

```
using System;
using System.Collections.Generic;
using System.IO;
using System.Linq;
using System.Text;
```

```csharp
using System.Threading.Tasks;
using System.Collections;

namespace MyProgram
{
    class Program
    {
        static void Main(string[] args)
        {

            Stack newstack = new Stack();
            newstack.Push(true);
            newstack.Push(20);
            newstack.Push("Hello");
            newstack.Push(1.56);


Console.WriteLine(newstack.Peek());

Console.WriteLine(newstack.Peek());

            Console.ReadLine();
        }

    }

}
```

In the script above, we call the Peek() method twice which will return 1.56 twice since it is the last item in the stack. The output looks like this:

C:\Users\Admin\source\repos\MyPrc

```
1.56
1.56
```

Another way to access elements from a Stack is by using the Pop(). The Pop() method removes the last item from the stack and returns the item to the calling function. Calling Pop() method twice returns last two elements from the stack. Take a look at the following example:

```csharp
using System;
using System.Collections.Generic;
using System.IO;
using System.Linq;
using System.Text;
using System.Threading.Tasks;
using System.Collections;

namespace MyProgram
{
    class Program
    {
        static void Main(string[] args)
```

```
        {

                Stack newstack = new Stack();
                newstack.Push(true);
                newstack.Push(20);
                newstack.Push("Hello");
                newstack.Push(1.56);


                Console.WriteLine(newstack.Pop());
                Console.WriteLine(newstack.Pop());

                Console.WriteLine(newstack.Count);

                Console.ReadLine();

        }

    }

}
```

In the script above, the Pop() method is called twice which returns 1.56 and "Hello" since these are the last two items in the Stack. Next, we count the number of items in the Stack which should return 2 since there were a total of four items and we removed 2 of them using the Pop() method.

245

Finally, you can use a foreach loop to iterate through the items in a stack as shown below:

```
using System;
using System.Collections.Generic;
using System.IO;
using System.Linq;
using System.Text;
using System.Threading.Tasks;
using System.Collections;

namespace MyProgram
{
    class Program
    {
        static void Main(string[] args)
        {

            Stack newstack = new Stack();
            newstack.Push(true);
            newstack.Push(20);
            newstack.Push("Hello");
            newstack.Push(1.56);
```

```
            foreach (var item in newstack)
                Console.WriteLine(item);

            Console.ReadLine();
        }

    }

}
```

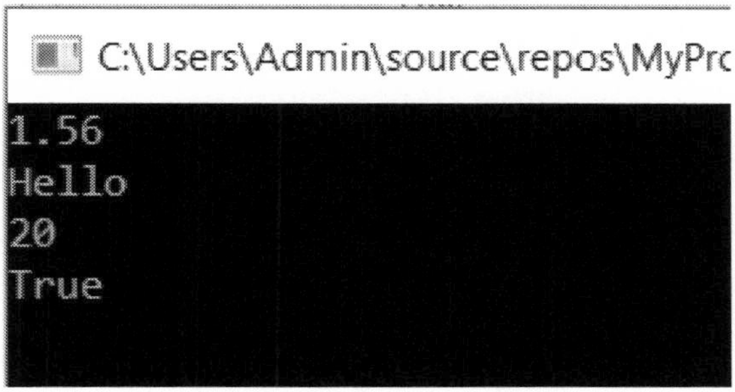

Clearing the Stack

You can clear a Stack using the Clear() function as shown below:

```
using System;
using System.Collections.Generic;
using System.IO;
using System.Linq;
using System.Text;
using System.Threading.Tasks;
```

```csharp
using System.Collections;

namespace MyProgram
{
    class Program
    {
        static void Main(string[] args)
        {

            Stack newstack = new Stack();
            newstack.Push(true);
            newstack.Push(20);
            newstack.Push("Hello");
            newstack.Push(1.56);

            Console.WriteLine("Elements before
clearing the stack:" + newstack.Count);
            newstack.Clear();
            Console.WriteLine("Elements after
clearing the stack:" + newstack.Count);

            Console.ReadLine();
        }

    }
}
```

In the script above, print the number of items in a stack before and after clearing the stack. The output of the script above looks like this:

```
C:\Users\Admin\source\repos\MyProgram\MyProgram\bin\
Elements before clearing the stack:4
Elements after clearing the stack:0
```

You can see that before we cleared the stack there were 4 items in the list and after we cleared the stack, we have zero items in the list.

Queue

The Queue is used to store elements in the form of FIFI (first in first out). Let's see some commonly used Queue functions

Creating a Queue

To create a Queue, you can use the **new** keyword followed by the class name "Queue" as shown below:

```
using System;
using System.Collections.Generic;
using System.IO;
using System.Linq;
using System.Text;
using System.Threading.Tasks;
```

```
using System.Collections;

namespace MyProgram
{
    class Program
    {
        static void Main(string[] args)
        {

            Queue newqueue = new Queue();

            Console.ReadLine();
        }
    }
}
```

Adding Elements to a Queue

To add elements to a Queue, you can use the Enqueue()
method as shown below:

```
using System;
using System.Collections.Generic;
using System.IO;
using System.Linq;
using System.Text;
using System.Threading.Tasks;
```

```csharp
using System.Collections;

namespace MyProgram
{
    class Program
    {
        static void Main(string[] args)
        {

            Queue newqueue = new Queue();

            newqueue.Enqueue(true);
            newqueue.Enqueue(10);
            newqueue.Enqueue("hello");
            newqueue.Enqueue(1.65);


            Console.ReadLine();

        }

    }
}
```

In the script above, we add four elements to the Queue.

Accessing Elements from Queue

To access elements from a Queue, you can use Peek() or Dequeue() methods. The Peek() method returns the first element from the Queue, whereas Dequeue()

removes and returns the first item from the Queue. Take a look at the following example.

```
using System;
using System.Collections.Generic;
using System.IO;
using System.Linq;
using System.Text;
using System.Threading.Tasks;
using System.Collections;

namespace MyProgram
{
    class Program
    {
        static void Main(string[] args)
        {

            Queue newqueue = new Queue();

            newqueue.Enqueue(true);
            newqueue.Enqueue(10);
            newqueue.Enqueue("hello");
            newqueue.Enqueue(1.65);
```

```
Console.WriteLine(newqueue.Peek());

Console.WriteLine(newqueue.Dequeue());

        Console.WriteLine(newqueue.Count);

        Console.ReadLine();

    }

  }

}
```

In the script above, we use the Peek() method to return the first element which will be "true". Next, we use the Dequeue() method to return the first element which will again return "true" but it will remove the first element from the list as well. Next, we count the number of elements in our Queue which should be 3 now since one of the items have been removed. The output of the script above looks like this:

In addition to Peek() and Dequeue() method to access the items in a Queue, you can use a foreach loop to iterate through each item in the Queue. You will need to convert the Queue into an array using the ToArray() method as shown below:

```csharp
using System;
using System.Collections.Generic;
using System.IO;
using System.Linq;
using System.Text;
using System.Threading.Tasks;
using System.Collections;

namespace MyProgram
{
    class Program
    {
        static void Main(string[] args)
        {

            Queue newqueue = new Queue();

            newqueue.Enqueue(true);
            newqueue.Enqueue(10);
            newqueue.Enqueue("hello");
            newqueue.Enqueue(1.65);
```

```
            foreach (var item in
newqueue.ToArray())

            Console.WriteLine(item);


        Console.ReadLine();

    }

  }

}
```

In the script above, we iterate through all the items in the Queue "newqueue". The output of the script above, looks like this:

■ C:\Users\Admin\source\repos\MyProgram\M

```
True
10
hello
1.65
```

Clearing a Queue

To remove all the items from a Queue, you can use the clear method as shown below:

```csharp
using System;
using System.Collections.Generic;
using System.IO;
using System.Linq;
using System.Text;
using System.Threading.Tasks;
using System.Collections;

namespace MyProgram
{
    class Program
    {
        static void Main(string[] args)
        {

            Queue newqueue = new Queue();

            newqueue.Enqueue(true);
            newqueue.Enqueue(10);
            newqueue.Enqueue("hello");
            newqueue.Enqueue(1.65);

            Console.WriteLine(newqueue.Count);

            newqueue.Clear();

            Console.WriteLine(newqueue.Count);

            Console.ReadLine();
```

```
        }
    }
}
```

In the script above we have four items in the Queue.
We print the number of items in the Queue before and
after calling the Clear() method. You will see that 0 will
be printed on the console after you clear the Queue and
print its number of items as shown below:

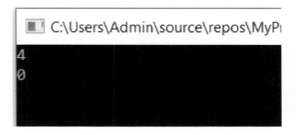

Checking if Queue Contains an Element

To check if a Queue contains a specific element, you can
make use of the Contains() method as shown below:

```
using System;
using System.Collections.Generic;
using System.IO;
using System.Linq;
using System.Text;
using System.Threading.Tasks;
```

```csharp
using System.Collections;

namespace MyProgram
{
    class Program
    {
        static void Main(string[] args)
        {

            Queue newqueue = new Queue();

            newqueue.Enqueue(true);
            newqueue.Enqueue(10);
            newqueue.Enqueue("hello");
            newqueue.Enqueue(1.65);


Console.WriteLine(newqueue.Contains(10));

Console.WriteLine(newqueue.Contains(20));

            Console.ReadLine();
        }
    }
}
```

In the script above we check if the Queue contains item 10 which returns true. Next, we check if the Queue contains 20, which returns false as shown in the output:

Conclusion

In this chapter, we studied C# collections in detail. We studied what are the different types of C# collections including ArrayList, SortedList, Stack, and Queue. We also saw the most commonly used methods on these collections. And with that, the book ends. From here, you can use the knowledge gained in this book to create your own C# applications including ASP.NET backend applications, mobile applications, and desktop applications.

Made in the USA
Middletown, DE
22 September 2019

69770205R00158